I0026751

Theory on Demand #43
Freire and the Perseverance of Hope — Exploring Communication and Social Change

Edited by Ana Cristina Suzina & Thomas Tufte.

Authors: Ailton Krenak, Ana Cristina Suzina, Anita Gurumurthy, Benjamin Ferron, Claudia Magallanes-Blanco, Colin Chasi, Elijerton Veras, Eriberto Gualinga Montalvo, Fania Sánchez de la Vega González, Frei Betto, Happy Singu Hansen, James Deane, Jharna Brahma, Karin Gwinn Wilkins, Linje Manyozo, Mayrá Lima, Michael Dokyum Kim, Nompumelelo 'Mpume' Gumede, Thomas Tufte, Xavier Carbonell.

Cover design: Katja van Stiphout
Design and production: Maria van der Togt
Publisher: Institute of Network Cultures, Amsterdam, 2022

ISBN print-on-demand: 9789492302847
ISBN EPUB: 9789492302854

Contact

Institute of Network Cultures
Email: info@networkcultures.org
Web: http://www.networkcultures.org

Download this publication free of charge or order a copy at
http://networkcultures.org/publications.

institute of
network cultures

**Loughborough
University**
London

PRAISE FOR THE BOOK

Echoing the words of Frei Betto in this book's first chapter, "I can say without fear of exaggeration" that my career in the field of communication for social change began when I read Pedagogy of the Oppressed in Colombia in 1982 at the age of twenty-two. As I was becoming more and more disillusioned with the media's potential to facilitate justice and equality, finding Paulo Freire meant recovering hope. Freire's invitation to understand political agency as a product of lived experience, language, and communication suggested a new path for thinking about and using communication toward social change. I welcome this book as an excellent resource for introducing my students to key Freirean notions such as the reality that activist knowledge has to emerge from the lived experiences of local communities; language is valuable only if it allows us to speak the world in our own terms; language rooted in lived experience and engaged in collective dialogue forms the basis of political awareness and activist mobilization; and the truth that love, empathy, humility, and creativity are essential to social movements. As the chapters in this book demonstrate, Freire's ideas have great potential for dialogue with Indigenous epistemologies, notions of Ubuntu, theatre of the oppressed in India, educational initiatives in Tanzania . . . the sky is the limit!

Clemencia Rodríguez, Professor, Director of the MSP Master of Arts Program, Department of Media Studies and Production, Klein College of Media and Communication, Temple University, United States

It is quite extraordinary that 25 years after Freire's death, his core values of dialogue, love, empathy, hope and humility continue to inform and shape creative practices of communications and knowledge making throughout our world. Weaving intellectual conversations with practical insights from the field, experiential knowledge with communitarian visions, this volume highlights the centrality of Freirean ideas at the core of communications for social change.

Pradip Thomas, University of Queensland, Australia

This timely book's 'back to the future' uniqueness is provided through renowned social change scholars, activists and practitioners 'looking back' on the positive influence Freire has had on their work. The future is illuminated through the refreshing inclusion of doctoral students whose emerging research provides a hopeful forecasting of Freire's continued relevance. Ideas are quilted together to provide a colorful, multivocal and multicultural exposition of the prescience of Freire's ideas for addressing today's societal concerns. The book is a testament to the potentiality of Freire's five human-centered ontological principles in guiding pro-social transformation through the iterative process of action and reflection. It's structure and style mirrors Freire's dialogic conscientization through the production of an empathetic knowledge of people's experiences and values; inviting a diverse readership to identify with stories and insights and enriching our understanding of people and contexts that may be different to one's own.

Lauren Dyll, Associate Professor, The Centre for Communication, Media and Society in the School of Applied Human Sciences, University of KwaZulu-Natal, South Africa

When speaking of the heretical heritage of Latin America in fields such as education and communication, and in the social sciences in general, it is not suggested that concepts such as emancipation, social change, politics, culture, emotions, feelings, have not been taken up again, in other latitudes, from the Latin American perspective. However, although these notions are mobilized in a segregated way in the global north, the greatest potential of this heritage is that in our continent these concepts have been born and have been experienced together in a kind of feeling-thinking: reason and feelings combined in a political perspective of social transformation. The legacy of Paulo Freire, one of the backbones of this heritage, as pointed out in the book, proposes: "a vindication of affection as resistance and as the central axis of social change." Throughout the book, through *dialogues* (conferences and debates), *empathy* (different territorial perspectives), *humility* (diversity of voices), and *love* (nostalgic celebration and vindication), Freire's ontological/epistemological call is taken up, understanding that the validity of his thought is more in his questions than in his answers and that *hope* would be in the way we assume them.

Jair Vega, Professor of Communication and Politics and member of PBX, Communication, Culture and Social Change Research Group, Department of Social Communication, Universidad del Norte, Barranquilla, Colombia

This wide-ranging and important volume offers meaningful perspectives and entry-points to the work of Freire that are relevant to contemporary critical design scholarship and practice. Freire's ideas offer directions to redress rampant instrumentalism in and of design, instrumentalism evident in the ways in which design is implicated in the design of digital communication products, services, infrastructures, and institutions, which in their current formations only serve to marginalise and oppress certain groups or populations. Engaging with Freire's thought opens pathways to revitalise and radicalise the oftentimes staid, normative and idealistic ways in which design engages with concepts such as hope, empathy, dialogue, and participation—concepts dealt with throughout this book—towards new articulations of design as a liberatory human capacity and social practice. 'Reclaiming Affect in Resistance—a Freirean Manifesto for Communication and Social Change', provides many and various touchpoints through which critical design scholars can take up this task.

Sharon Prendeville, Senior Lecturer/Associate Professor, Programme Director of the MSc Design Innovation Management, Institute of Design Innovation, Loughborough University, London, United Kingdom

Paulo Freire's centenary was celebrated in Brazil, his country of origin, with many ceremonies, congresses, and publications. In the context which the country is experiencing, with a setback in so many areas, all this celebration represented an encouragement. However, it must be recognized that these celebrations began at Loughborough University in March 2019 with a preliminary seminar. This book masterfully brings together the participation in the great seminar held in March 2021, which brought together theorists from all over the world. It is exciting to read Paulo Freire based on experiences and interpretations that reaffirm the relevance of his thinking. This is a book that will certainly be a reference for the celebration of Freire's 200 years.

Raquel Paiva, Emeritus Professor at Federal University of Rio de Janeiro, Visiting Professor at State University of Rio de Janeiro, Researcher at National Research Council, Brazil

This important collection is a must-read for everyone interested in how the influential work of Paulo Freire translates to the challenges of today's complex society. Promoting a diverse and urgent dialogue amongst a multiplicity of experts, geographical sites, and thematic foci, it future-proofs Freire's ideas and principles, making them not only relevant but also indispensable to our efforts to understand and reform contemporaneity.

Stefania Milan, Professor of Critical Data Studies, University of Amsterdam

ACKNOWLEDGEMENTS

Making this book a reality has been the result of a collective process to which we own many people and institutions our thanks. Loughborough University's Joint Fund supported the initial seminar in June 2019 that kick-started our involvement with Freirean centenary celebrations. We are also grateful to Loughborough University for supporting the organization of the seminar *Paulo Freire Centennial: 7 Talks in Preparation for the Next 100 Years* during a period of contention due to the evolution of the pandemics, in March 2021.

We thank all the 856 individual participants, from 42 countries, who enrolled in the seven dialogues, many in more than one of them. They prompted the reflections to meet current shared challenges faced in the conceptualization and practice of communication in processes of social change, highlighting the actuality and the radicality of Freire's thoughts.

Without the Brazilian NGO Ubiqua, responsible for a lot of the logistics around our March 2021 seminar, we would not have had recordings to work with. Ubiqua secured the recordings we edited and worked with for sections 1 and 2 of this book. Our gratitude and admiration for the great and committed work of Jessé Barbosa, Eulália Vasconcelos, Margella Furtado, Walton Luz, Márcio Bigly and all their teams. We are furthermore immensely thankful to Jim McDonnel, Fernanda Amaral and Susan Weissert for their work with transcription, translation, and language review.

We are also very thankful to all contributors for their participation in the seminar, for their texts, and for engaging with us in the editorial process. We appreciate their open and critical posture that makes this collection diverse and still coherent.

Finally, we would like to thank Institute of Network Cultures, Geert Lovink and Isabel Lofgren in particular, for accepting this manuscript and patiently working with us on completing this publication, Maria van der Togt for her careful work in the design project, and the whole team involved in different tasks. It means a lot to see these debates among so many relevant ones covered by the series *Theory on Demand*, mainly confirming the significance of stating that dialogue, love, empathy, hope and humility can still illuminate our debates regarding the way we communicate, build knowledge and fight for change.

CONTENTS

SECTION 1 – REFLECTIONS ON FREIRE'S PRINCIPLES

SECTION 2 – DEBATING FREIRE'S IDEAS

INTRODUCTION: WHY AND HOW TO READ THIS BOOK

ANA CRISTINA SUZINA AND THOMAS TUFTE

In March 2021, the Institute for Media and Creative Industries at Loughborough University London organized a cycle called *Paulo Freire Centennial: 7 Talks in Preparation for the Next 100 years*. It was an early step towards Freire's birth centennial to be celebrated in September of that same year. The event got more than six thousand submissions for participation in its seven dialogues – 2.113 individual submissions from 48 countries, being the first thousand in the first six hours after opening registration. Aware of hate campaigns against Freire, those submissions were double checked and, for confirming a place in the debates, subscribers were requested to fill in a form and, among other questions, answer what they were looking for. Many summarized that, at that point, "Freire was more necessary than ever". Filtering numbers, 856 individual participants from 42 countries enrolled in the seven dialogues, many in more than one of them.

The collection of texts organized in this book comes from those seven debates. Twelve speakers, from 10 countries, representing experience from both research and practice in communication and social change, discussed the five principles of Freire's ontological call: dialogue, love, empathy, hope and humility.[1] Section 1 of this book contains the integral transcriptions of these lectures – some of them are direct translations to English as speakers addressed the public in their original languages.

Section 2 is comprised of another group of transcriptions from the dialogues. In this case, the live debates that took place after each lecture were transcribed and organized under topics that unfolded between speakers and the audience. We have organized these around the three main topics that emerged in the debates: Network Society; Social Change; and Education. They are in turn internally organized under subtopics.

Finally, Section 3 is comprised of a collection of texts written by young communication scholars and practitioners that attended the cycle. They write from their local perspective about how those discussions inspired or challenged their work and views of the future.

In the epilogue, we offer our perspective of the year of celebrations around Freire's birth centennial – it is based on our participations in a number of events, and our monitoring and observation of many more. Between the spirits of nostalgia and the will of finding inspiration for current and future challenges, we observed exercises of both memory and reinvention. From our engagement with this centennial celebration of the birth of Paulo Freire, we can affirm that the reason that makes reading Freire today relevant is that his work still sparks the fire of searching and fighting for the human in all our communication processes.

---

1   Paulo Freire, Pedagogia do Oprimido, São Paulo, Paz e Terra, 2017; Ana Cristina Suzina and Thomas Tufte. 'Freire's vision of development and social change: Past experiences, present challenges and perspectives for the future', International Communication Gazette, 82, 5 (2020).

While admiring the resonance the centennial celebrations of Paulo Freire have had amongst a broad gamut of change agents and academics across the globe, and while taking pleasure in paying tribute to and remembering one of the most important social scientists and humanists of the 21st century, one of our key concerns in celebrating Freire and publishing this book has been to discuss the relevance of his ideas for the problems and challenges of the digital age. Are networks emancipating people or increasing relations of domination? Is technology empowering voice or deepening the silence we also see proliferating? How do Freire's ontological principles connect with these kinds of questions? How does Freire's entire work connect with the communicative practice of the digital age? In editing this book, we have seen a broad set of answers to this question, and we pick upon some of these in the post-face of the book. At this stage, we wish you a pleasurable read and hope the books proves relevant and useful to your research or practice.

References

Ana Cristina Suzina and Thomas Tufte. 'Freire's vision of development and social change: Past experiences, present challenges and perspectives for the future', International Communication Gazette, 82, 5 (2020): 411-424.

Paulo Freire, Pedagogia do Oprimido, São Paulo, Paz e Terra, 2017.

List of works published as outcomes from Loughborough University's Freire-related activities:

In Portuguese and English:

Paulo Freire Centennial: 7 Talks in Preparation for the Next 100 Years (video recording of the lectures): https://repository.lboro.ac.uk/projects/Paulo_Freire_Centennial_7_Talks_in_Preparation_for_the_Next_100_Years/111428.

Dossier Paulo Freire, 100 anos. Revista Matrizes, v.15, n. 3 (octubre / diciembre de 2021): https://www.revistas.usp.br/matrizes.

In English:

Special Issue 2020: Freire's vision of development and social change – past experiences, present challenges and perspectives for the future. International Communication Gazette, 82: 5, August: https://journals.sagepub.com/toc/gazb/82/5.

In Spanish and English:

Special Issue 2020: The legacy of Paulo Freire. Roles and challenges of Social Movements. Commons. Revista de Comunicación y Ciudadanía Digital, 9(2): https://revistas.uca.es/index.php/cayp/issue/view/432https://revistas.uca.es/index.php/cayp/issue/view/432.

In Spanish and Portuguese:

Revista Punto de Encuentro: Edición Conmemorativa del Centenario de Paulo Freire: https://signisalc.org/producto/encuentros-paulofreire-comunicacion/.

In Portuguese:

Suzina, A.C., Tufte, T. & Jiménez-Martínez, C. (2020). Qual a mensagem de Paulo Freire para os días atuais?: diálogos sobre a relevância do pensamento de Freire para entender o Brasil hoje. Revista Internacional de Comunicación y Desarrollo, 11, 11-18: https://revistas.usc.gal/index.php/ricd/article/view/6543.

In French:

Suzina, A.C. (2021). Paulo Freire: La voie/voix collective de l'émancipation. Revue Démocratie. MOC: August 2021. http://www.revue-democratie.be/index.php?option=com_content&view=article&id=1509:paulo-freire-la-voie-voix-collective-de-l-emancipation&catid=15&Itemid=148.

SECTION 1 – REFLECTIONS ON FREIRE'S PRINCIPLES

This section reproduces the transcription of the 12 lectures delivered during the cycle *Paulo Freire Centennial: 7 Talks in Preparation for the Next 100 years*[1]. Those delivered in other languages were translated into English. Those delivered in English were reviewed and slightly edited by own authors and a language reviewer in order to adapt oral language to the written one. The videos of the lectures are still available, subtitled in English and/or Portuguese, accordingly. They can be found at:

https://repository.lboro.ac.uk/projects/Paulo_Freire_Centennial_7_Talks_in_Preparation_for_the_Next_100_Years/111428.

---

[1] Language review for English translations provided by Jim McDonnel.

HOMAGE TO PAULO FREIRE ON HIS CENTENARY

FREI BETTO

I can say without fear of exaggeration that Paulo Freire is the root of the history of Brazilian popular power in the 50 years between 1966 and 2016 - 2016 because that was when the parliamentary coup toppled President Dilma Rousseff from the presidency of the Republic. This power emerged as a leafy tree from the Brazilian active left in the second half of the twentieth century: groups that fought against the military dictatorship (1964-1985); the CEBs (*Comunidades Ecleciais de Base,* Basic Ecclesial Communities of the Christian Churches); the large network of popular and social movements that emerged in the 70s; the combative unionism that emerged since 1975; and, in the 1980s, this whole process of accumulating forces of popular power summed up with the foundation of CUT (*Central Única dos Trabalhadores,* Unified Workers Union); of ANAMPOS (*Articulacao Nacional dos Movimentos Populares e Sindicais,* National Articulation of Popular and Trade Union Movements), the creation of PT (*Partido dos Trabalhadores,* Workers' Parties); and, subsequently, in the 1990s led to the creation of CMP (*Central de Movimentos Populares,* Central of Popular Movements); the MST (*Movimento dos Trabalhadores Rurais Sem Terra,* Landless Rural Workers Movement); and so many other movements, NGOs and entities that are part of what I call popular power.

If I had to respond to the question 'Point out a person in the origins of all of this', I would say, without any doubt: Paulo Freire. Without the popular education methodology of Paulo Freire, there would not be these movements because he taught us something very important: to see history, to face history from the perspective of the oppressed and make them protagonists of change in society.

The popular power

I was in prison for four years during the military dictatorship, from 1969 to 1973, and when, at the end of 1973, I left the prison, I had the impression that every social struggle out there had ended under the repression of the military dictatorship. Because I was still imbued with that elitist mentality that we, petty-bourgeois intellectuals, are the ones who teach the people what to do and, therefore, I said, 'the people cannot mobilize because we are either imprisoned, or we were murdered, or we live in exile'.

What was my surprise when I found an immense network of popular and social movements, that is, a network that had spread throughout Brazil since the early 1960s and was reinforced during the period of the military dictatorship, first by the Basic Ecclesial Communities - not least because the repression did not give them much attention, saying that it was a religious movement that did not represent danger, without realizing the progressive character that they had and still have.

When PT was founded in 1980, I saw fellow left-wingers react, 'Workers willing to have their own party? No. It is a lot of pretentious.'

We, the petty-bourgeois, intellectuals, academics, Marxist theorists have always been at the forefront of the proletariat. What pretense is it now that the proletarians want to be their own vanguard? It is a little ironic, but it is an irony that is supported by facts. And, in fact, at this turn from the1970s to 1980s, the dictatorship began to weaken because precisely this process of accumulation of popular forces led it to be weakened and this process is due to the methodology of Paulo Freire.

Once in Mexico, comrades from the left asked me:

- How can we do something similar to your process in Brazil? Why do you have a left-wing sector in the Church, a combative union, the PT? How do you get this popular political force?

- Start doing popular education - I replied - and in forty years ...

They interrupted me:

- Forty years is a lot! We want a suggestion for four years.

- In four years, I don't know how to do it.

In short, the whole process of building up popular political forces, which resulted in the election of Lula as president of Brazil in 2002 and kept the PT in the federal government for thirteen years, everything was built through the application of the Paulo Freire's method.

Encounters with Freire's method

I got to know the Paulo Freire method in 1963. I lived in Rio de Janeiro; I was part of the national leadership of Catholic Action. When the first working groups of the Paulo Freire method appeared, I joined a team that, during the weekends, went up to Petrópolis, 70km from Rio, to teach workers at the National Motor Factory in a church hall.

We photographed the facilities, gathered the workers, projected slides and asked an absolutely simple question:

- In this photo, what *didn't* you *do*?

- Well, *we didn't* make the tree, the forest, the dirt road, the water ...

What you didn't make is nature, we said.

- And what did human work *do*? - we asked.

- Human work made the brick, the factory, the bridge, the fence ...

This is culture, we said. - And how were these things done?

They debated and replied:

- They were made as humans transformed nature into culture.

Then there was a picture of the yard of the National Motor Factory occupied by many trucks and the workers' bicycles. We simply asked:

- In this photo, what did you make?

- The trucks.

- And what do you have?

- The bikes.

- Couldn't you be wrong? You say you make the trucks, but you own the bikes.

- No, we manufacture trucks. But the truck is expensive, and it doesn't belong to us.

- How much does a truck cost?

- About 40 thousand dollars.

- How much do you earn per month?

- Well, we earn an average of 200 dollars.

- How long do each of you have to work, without eating, without drinking, without paying rent, saving all earnings to, one day, own the truck that you make?

They began to calculate and became aware of the nature of the relationship of capital x working, which is surplus value, exploitation etc. And it was the generative themes that allowed the literacy process.

The most elementary notions of Marxism as a critique of capitalism came through their own experience thanks to the Paulo Freire method. With the difference that we were not teaching, we did not do what Paulo Freire called 'banking education', that is, putting academic, abstract notions in the head of the worker. No, it was always from the context, from their reality.

When I came to São Bernardo do Campo (SP), in 1980, I worked there in the Workers Pastorate for 22 years, there were militants of the left who distributed newspapers among the families of the workers. One day, Marta asked me:

- What is *crass* contradiction?

- Dona Marta, forget that.

- I don't read much - she justified herself- because my sight is bad and the letters, small.

Forget it, I said. - The left writes these texts for it to read and be happy with, and not for people to understand.

Paulo Freire taught us to speak in popular language. Popular language is plastic, it is not academic, it is not abstract, it is not conceptual. When the people speak, we see what the people say. I usually say that this is why the Bible is so popular, because the Bible does not have a single lesson in theology or doctrine; all of them are plastic descriptions. When you read it, you see the narrative; it's like a novel. This is very important in the language of the Paulo Freire method; adopt the popular language itself.

Upon leaving prison, by the end of 1973, I lived for five years in a slum in the city of Vitória, Espírito Santo. There was a group of women pregnant with their first child, assisted by doctors from the Municipal Health Department. I asked the doctors why they worked only with women pregnant with their first child. We do not want women who already have maternal habits, he answered.

Well, a few months later, one of the doctors, Dr Raul, knocked on the door of my hut.

- Betto, we want your help. There is problem between us and the women. They don't understand what we say. You, who have experience with popular education, could advise us.

I went to the community center to watch their work. When I entered the health center, I saw the distance between the doctors and the women. The Centre was completely decorated with posters of Johnson babies, blondes with blue eyes, Nestlé milk propaganda etc. When women come in here, they realize that this has nothing to do with the reality in the slum.

I realized that the doctors were speaking in Modulated Frequency, but the women were tuned to Medium Wave.

Then I asked Dona Maria: Did you understand what Dr Raul said?

- Almost nothing. Because I don't have an education. I didn't attend school much; I was born poor in the countryside. I had to work on the plantations and help support the family. I just understood that he says that our milk is good for children's heads.

So, I asked Dr Raul, in front of the women, if he knew how to cook.

- Do you know how to make chicken with brown sauce (a dish that, in Espírito Santo, and in some areas of the Northeast, is called *cabidela* chicken)?

- No. In the kitchen, I can't even boil an egg.

Then, I asked Dona Maria again: Do you know how to make chicken with brown sauce?

- I do.

- Please, stand up - I asked - and tell us how to make a chicken with brown sauce.

Dona Maria gave a cooking class: how to kill the chicken, which side the feathers are taken from, how to prepare the meat and make the sauce etc.

When she sat down, I said:

- Dona Maria if you and Doctor Raul are both lost and hungry in a dense forest, and, suddenly, a chicken appears, he, with all his culture, dies hungry and, you do not.

The woman smiled openly. She discovered, at that moment, a fundamental principle of Paulo Freire: there is no one more cultured than the other, there are distinct cultures, socially complementary.

What would be, for example, the nuclear physicist, the chemist, the theologian, who do not know how to cook, if culinary culture did not exist? If there was not a cook who is often semi-illiterate, but with a deep culinary culture to prepare their food?

So, this was very important: to rescue in the oppressed the culture they have, something they have but they often do not feel valued in it, they do not feel recognized in their knowledge. They know and often are not aware about how much they know, let alone the value of that knowledge.

A call from the grassroots

Given the emergence of so many authoritarian governments and the profusion in digital networks - which I refuse to call social, because they don't always create sociability and, therefore, I prefer to use the technical-digital name - of anti-democratic, racist, homophobic, sexist and denialist messages on digital networks, it seems to me of utmost importance to revisit Paulo Freire on this date of the centenary of his birth.

The retreat of progressive forces in Latin America in recent years, and the rise of neo-fascist figures such as Bolsonaro in Brazil, oblige us to recognize that we have abandoned the grassroots work of popular organization and mobilization for decades. This void with the populations of the periphery, the slums, the poor rural areas, has been occupied by religious fundamentalism, drug trafficking and militia.

In his works, Paulo Freire teaches us that there is no mobilization without prior awareness. It is necessary for people to be aware of their historical role, aware of the situation, of reality, to be able to mobilize. Aware even of the meaning of life. The meaning of existence is what makes us mobilize. We need people to have a *clothesline* on which to hang political and analytical concepts and the keys for analyzing reality. The *clothesline* is the perception of time as history.

If someone asks me what the main philosophical problem is today, I will say, without a doubt, it is precisely the de-historization of time.

There are civilizations, tribes, groups, which have no perception of time as history. Ancient Greeks, for example, believed that time is cyclical. Today, cyclical time returns through the denial, fatalism, and flat-Earth theories, but it returns, above all, due to neoliberalism.

The essence of neoliberalism is the *de-historization of time*. When Fukuyama declared 'the end of history',[1] he expressed what neoliberalism wants to instill: that we have reached the fullness of time! The neoliberal mode of capitalist production, based on the supremacy of the market, is definitive! A few are chosen and, many, excluded. The neoliberalism wants us to believe that there is no use wanting to fight for an alternative society, 'another world is possible'![2]

In fact, today it is difficult to speak of an alternative society. Socialism then, no way! Shame has emerged, an intellectual and emotional block. Even left wingers say that 'socialism collapsed, fell, was buried!' The alternatives that arise are generally intra-systemic, they are not alternatives that intend or aim to overcome the capitalist system.

This notion that *time is history* comes from the Persians, passed on to the Hebrews and accentuated by Jewish tradition through the Bible. It is fundamental to rescue this sense of historical vision and mobilization to change this process. Three great paradigms of our culture are of Jewish origin - Jesus, Marx and Freud - and the three had a strong root of historicity in their messages.

It is not possible to study Marxism without going deeply into the previous modes of production, to understand how the capitalist mode of production was established. And to understand, then, how its contradictions can lead to socialist and communist modes of production. Marxist analysis therefore assumes the rescue of time as history.

If someone undergoes psychological analysis or therapy, the psychoanalyst immediately asks the patient about their past, their childhood, their upbringing. If the patient can talk about their life in the womb, this will help a lot to restore their balance today, for a better life in the future.

Jesus' perspective was historical. The God of Jesus presents himself with a curriculum vitae: "I believe in the God of Abraham, Isaac and Jacob" - that is a whole line of historicity

---

1   In reference to Francis Fukuyama's 'The End of History and the Last Man', a 1992 book of political
     philosophy.
2   Slogan of the World Social Forum.

in the very proclamation of the faith. The main category of Jesus' preaching is historical: the Kingdom of God, which unfortunately was placed by the church in heaven, but in Jesus' head, was ahead in history, it was a civilizing political proposal. Jesus did not die of hepatitis in bed, nor of a camel disaster on a corner of Jerusalem. He was, like many of our comrades here, in Latin America, during the military dictatorship, he was arrested, tortured, tried by two political powers, and sentenced to the death penalty of the Romans, which is the cross. Why did he suffer such cruelty? Precisely because he dared, within Caesar's kingdom, to speak of another possible kingdom, which He called the kingdom of God. He was convicted of perversion. All of us Christians are disciples of a political prisoner.

It is curious that in the Bible, history, in the Genesis' account of the creation of the world, already appears marked by this historicity, because it took seven days.

For the Greeks, who had a cyclical perception of the world, it was absurd, because how can one believe in the omnipotence of a god who is not able to create like Nescafé, instant? He needs to work for six days and still gets tired and goes to the beach on the seventh. In other words, the Greeks did not capture this dimension of historicity that, in the Bible, curiously appears even before the appearance of the human being.

This prevailing concept, that history begins with the action of human beings on nature, is a restricted concept, it is a concept surpassed I would say, because there is a historicity that precedes the appearance of the human being. Today, this is confirmed by cosmology, with the entire process of evolution of the universe, from the big bang to our appearance of homo sapiens, which is very recent, 250 thousand years ago.

It is very important to recover this dimension of historicity, this '*clothesline*. This perspective does not suit neoliberalism. But you cannot do popular education without having the "clothesline" to hang the clothes, ideas, experiences, facts on ... This *clothesline* - as long as history - is key to visualize the social and political process. This also happens in the micro dimension of our lives. Why, today, so many have difficulty having life projects? How come young people reach 20 years old without the slightest idea about who they want to be or what to do in life? For many of them, everything is here and now.

Therefore, if we want to rescue Paulo Freire's legacy, the path is to return to grassroots work with the popular classes, adopting his method in a historical perspective, open to libertarian utopias and the democratic horizon. There is no salvation outside the people. And if we believe that democracy should, in fact, be the government of the people for the people and with the people, there is no alternative but to adopt the Freirian educational process that situates the oppressed as political and historical protagonists.

Farewell

When Paulo Freire returned from 15 years of exile, in August 1979, we met in São Paulo. We were neighbors, and we often visited each other. Our personal relationships became a lot closer, which allowed us to write a book mediated by the journalist Ricardo Kotscho; the book was titled *This school called life.*

Paulo became ill in 1997 and died on May 2 of that year. Before, he had asked me, already sick, to represent him in Havana, in the delivery of *Doctor Honoris Causa*, by the University of Cuba. Unfortunately, I was unable to attend because I was scheduled to travel to Palestine. But I was with him in the final moments, in the moments that I call *transvivenciação*, in May 1997. And right after that I wrote a text and I want to share here because I think it translates the entire methodology of Professor Paulo Freire.

Ivo saw the grape, taught the literacy manuals. But Professor Paulo Freire, with his method of raising awareness, made adults and children, in Brazil and in Guinea-Bissau, in India, in Nicaragua and in many other places, discover that Ivo didn't just see with his eyes, he also saw with his mind and wondered if grapes are nature or culture.

Ivo saw that the fruit is not the result of human work. It's Creation, it's nature. Paulo Freire taught Ivo that sowing grapes is human action in and about nature. And the hand, a multipurpose tool, awakes the potential of the fruit. Just as the human being was sown by nature in the years and years of evolution of the Universe.

Harvesting the grape, crushing it, and transforming it into wine is culture, Paulo Freire pointed out. Work humanizes nature and, when doing it, men and women become humanized. Work that establishes the relationship node, social life. Thanks to the Freire, who started his revolutionary pedagogy with workers from the 'Sesi' of Pernambuco, Ivo also saw that the grape is harvested by workers (so-called 'boias frias'), who earned little, and traded by intermediaries, who earn much more.

Ivo learned from Paulo that, even without knowing how to read, he is not an ignorant person. Before learning letters, Ivo knew how to build a house, brick by brick. The doctor, the lawyer, or the dentist, with all their study, are not able to build like Ivo. Paulo Freire taught Ivo that no one is more cultured than another, there are parallel, distinct cultures that complement each other in social life.

Ivo saw the grape and Paulo Freire showed him the bunches, the vine, the entire plantation. He taught Ivo that the reading of a text is more understandable the more the text is inserted in the context of the author and the reader. It is from this dialogical relationship between text and context that Ivo extracts the pretext to act. At the beginning and at the end of learning it is Ivo's praxis that matters. Praxis-theory-praxis, in an inductive process that makes the student a historical subject.

Ivo saw the grape and did not see the bird that, from above, sees the vine and does not see the grape. What Ivo sees is different from what the bird sees. Thus, Paulo Freire taught Ivo a fundamental principle of epistemology: the head thinks where the feet step. The unequal world can be read from the oppressor's point of view or from the point of view of the oppressed. It results in a reading as different one from another as between Ptolemy's vision, when observing the solar system with his feet on Earth, and Copernicus, when imagining himself with his feet in the Sun.

Now Ivo sees the grape, the vine and all the social relationships that make the fruit a party in the wine cup, but he no longer sees Paulo Freire, who died in God's Love on the morning of May 2, 1997. He leaves us with an invaluable work and an admirable testimony of competence and consistency.

Paulo was to be in Cuba, where he would receive the title of Doctor Honoris Causa, *from the University of Havana — and in which I could not represent him. However, before embarking to Palestine I went to pray with Nita, his wife, and their children around his calm face: Paulo saw God.*

A DIALOGUE ON COMMUNICATION FROM AN INDIGENOUS PERSPECTIVE IN MEXICO

CLAUDIA MAGALLANES-BLANCO

In December 2018, Indigenous communicators from different ethnic groups, facilitators of community processes and socially committed academics met in the city of Oaxaca, in the Southern state of the same name in Mexico. We gathered for two days to reflect upon our practices as media producers, researchers, and facilitators of communication processes. Using different participatory techniques, we revisited the history of Indigenous media and communication in Mexico as well as its challenges, outcomes, achievements, and needs. We also debated the role of Indigenous media and communication practitioners inside and outside their communities, the relationship with the Mexican state and the way to go about media and communication form an Indigenous perspective.

Reflecting upon that meeting, we were finding the words to analyze our reality in relation to Indigenous communication. We decided how to name our practices and how to name the world we inhabit from the shared perspective we had about the Mexican historical context, the living conditions of Indigenous communities throughout the territory and the media and communication practices displayed by different Indigenous collectives, media, and practitioners. We were representing the world according to us and not to the imposed dominant discourse. This way, over the course of two days, we jointly constructed an enunciation of the world of Indigenous communication in Mexico, which we then translated into a collective text, some parts of which I have taken up for this article.[1]

The text served as a witness to the process of dialogue and collective construction among those of us who share our work on Indigenous media and communication in Mexico. We first talked about the political and social environment we are living in. Then we discussed both the hopes and fears, doubts, and desires we had. We recognized the historical context as corrupt, violent, unpunished, insecure and with public policies that threaten Indigenous Peoples and territories.[2]

---

1   The original collectively produced text is entitled *El quehacer de la comunicación desde los pueblos originarios (O cómo no estamos meando fuera de la bacinica)* [The purpose of communication from Indigenous Peoples (Or how we are not pissing out of the potty)].

2   A few references to understand the reading of the context that we made are:
[ ]'En México hay más de 73 mil desaparecidos y más de 3 mil fosas clandestinas', *Animal Político*, 13 July 2020, https://www.animalpolitico.com/2020/07/mexico-73-mil-desaparecidos-fosas-clandestinas/#:~:text=Entre%20enero%20y%20junio%20de,de%20177%20mil%20844%20personas.
Rubén Aguilar, 'El asesinato de los ecologistas en México' *Animal Político*, 4 Augusto 2020, www.animalpolitico.com/lo-que-quiso-decir/el-asesinato-de-los-ecologistas-en-mexico.
Inés Durán Matute and Rocío Moreno, *La lucha por la vida frente a los megaproyectos en México*, México: Universidad de Guadalajara-CIESAS-Jorge Alonso, 2021.
EDUCA, A.C., *El Topil. Boletín de Análisis y reflexión Política*. Nueva Época No.42 (April, 2021).
Giovanna Gasparello, 'Autonomías indígenas en México: construir la paz en contextos violentos' *QuAderns-e Institut Català d' Antropologia* Número 21 (1) Año 2016.

Our discussion was based on a shared common understanding of the structural imbalance of power that permeates all aspects of life and that shapes the world-system in which we live as colonial,[3] patriarchal and capitalist.[4] We live under multiple asymmetries of power that are intersectional.[5] There are diverse ways of exercising power across gender, race, religion, social status, and the environments in which we live. There are lines of confrontation that persist in the world system, such as the one that divides the oppressors from the oppressed,[6] those who count from those who do not count, those who are on one side or the other of the abyssal line[7]. The persistence of structural power asymmetries and the struggles, movements and resistances connected to it reveal a crisis of the world-system, of its economic model and its related practices and institutions.[8]

In line with Freire's thoughts,[9] we believe communication is a key factor for the understanding and enunciation of the world. Words allow us to express ourselves. Expressing the world means problematizing the world, analyzing it critically from the specific contexts in which we live in order to see the totality of the system and to highlight inequalities and asymmetries of power. The expression of the world must be critical, but at the same time it must include desires, aspirations, dreams, hopes, the possibility of a different world. As the Zapatistas would say, 'a world where many worlds fit'.[10]

When we use words, symbols, communicative practices and communication and information technologies we engage in an ongoing process of action and reflection. This is what Freire referred to as the praxis of the true word. The flow between action and reflection allows us to understand the changing reality and to identify the structures that are maintained, and those that should be transformed. For example, our communication practices are an alternative to the training we receive from school education. Community, Indigenous and popular communication, materialized in media outlets, messages and practices, is a school of life that generates an alternative model of education. This model allows us to re-educate ourselves and re-signify, with a critical sense, the symbolic and community elements that are substantive for life. It shows more dignified views of who we are based on ours words, detaching us from the colonizing language. This re-education also means strengthening ourselves politically, having greater elements of analysis of the realities we live to improve our dialogic capacity

---

Carmen Morán Breña, 'La violencia en México renueva cotas mortíferas en marzo', *El País*. 01 April 2021, https://elpais.com/mexico/2021-04-01/la-violencia-en-mexico-renueva-cotas-mortiferas-en-marzo.html.

3   Aníbal Quijano, 'Coloniality of power and Eurocentrism in Latin America' *International Sociology* 15.2 (2000).

4   Boaventura De Sousa Santos, *Epistemologies of the South: Justice Against Epistemicide*, London: Routledge, 2015.

5   Patricia Hill Collins and Sirma Bilge, *Intersectionality*, Cambridge: Polity Press, 2020.

6   Paulo Freire, *Pedagogy of the Oppressed*. Bloomsbury publishing USA, 2018.

7   Boaventura de Sousa Santos, 'Beyond Abyssal Thinking: From Global Lines to Ecologies of Knowledges' *Review* (Fernand Braudel Center) 2007.

8   María Eugenia Sánchez Díaz de Rivera (coord.), *Desgarramientos Civilizatorios. Símbolos, corporeidades, territorios*, Puebla: Universidad Iberoamericana Puebla, 2021.

9   Paulo Freire, *Pedagogy of the Oppressed*.

10   Slogan attributed to the Zapatist Movement, in Mexico.

with multiple social actors.

Communication allows us to recognize ourselves, to represent ourselves according to our codes and symbols. It makes us feel part of life in the territories through our daily activities, which include the reproduction of life, the preservation of culture and language as well as the struggles and resistances to different menaces we face. Part of that resistance is to fight for our right to exercise both individual and collective communication rights. Our different communication practices contribute to the self-determination of Indigenous Peoples through informing, triggering processes of reflection, training, community analysis, recovering historical memory, strengthening community structures, and appropriating different technologies to produce both mediated and non-mediated messages.

The praxis of the true word, the flow of action and reflection, has led us to recognize that although we are all different, we should not be unequal. Being aware of the many oppressions we live under should lead us to build different paths for emancipation. Liberation of the oppressed implies the rupture of the system and its power relations. One way to approach liberation is through a loving and dialogic commitment. As Freire said, authentic dialogue means the acknowledgment of the other and of oneself in the other. It is a conscious decision and commitment to work together in the construction of a shared world.[11] Through our media and communication practices we are building a shared world where Indigenous peoples' knowledge, practices, territories, languages, and cultures have the same value and relevance as those from the oppressors.

The way we approach communication practices cannot pigeonhole *the Indigenous*. We produce different messages and respect traditional forms of communication. We communicate with, for and from Indigenous traditions, costumes, and cultures. Our goals and ways of naming the world and of self-representing belong to us and not to the ongoing colonial powers. Our communication practices are deeply rooted in our territories, histories, and cultures. They are proper to the Indigenous People, hence, at its core are our ways of naming life, our ancestral wisdoms, traditions, languages, and identities. At the same time, we are aware that we need to have a critical understanding of our ancestry and costumes. We need to question and challenge those aspects of our cultures that reproduce power asymmetries to revert them. For example, we need to put a diverse and intergenerational dialogue at the forefront. To open a dialogue with children and youth, with disability, sexual diversity, women, and the elderly. This critical dialogue must be culturally anchored and must be a constant exercise in thinking and rethinking life in the territories, our role in the world-system and our relationship with other species. Dialogue happens from multiple forms of communications between and with different living beings, with the species with which we share this planet. We live in an imbalance with the different species, so we must bring dialogue to that dimension as well.

Freire argued that dialogue is a horizontal process that takes place on equal terms, that does not aim at homogenization, but at maintaining differences without inequity. It is a horizontal

---

11   Paulo Freire, *Pedagogy of the Oppressed.*

relationship to break the cycles of domination, segmentation, hierarchization, discrimination in a collaborative way, using communication. Dialogue is central to change. For those who participated at the meeting on Oaxaca at the end of 2018, dialogue is deeply connected to living, to defending life and to celebrating it. Through our dialogue between different Indigenous Peoples, media and communication initiatives, scholars, and even government agencies we recognized the contributions of Indigenous Peoples to Mexican society, culture and economy while at the same time we fight against racism, discrimination, invisibilization and lack of tolerance.[12] It is therefore necessary to continue to fight for diverse communication channels that allow us to make our ways of understanding and enunciating the world known. In this way we hope the country can feel proud of the Indigenous Peoples and thus contribute to the fight against racism and oppression.

We need to deeply reflect about the relationship we, as Indigenous Peoples have and want to have with the State. This is not an easy conversation as we have different perspectives, but at the meeting in Oaxaca we managed to have a respectful, loving, ethical and empathetic dialogue about it. We identified that we must strategically demand permanent access to the spaces that belong to us, such as telecommunications and communication and information technologies not only as receivers, but as producers. We also discussed the need to seek non-violent, proactive, and constructive dialogues with different state entities. We want the opinions of Indigenous Peoples included in decision-making processes to achieve changes in public policies. We want to re-shape the media discourses about Indigenous Peoples. We demand to exercise our right to communication having our media and communication technologies such as radio stations, video projects, digital media, intranets, and mobile communications networks.

We thought of strategies to give continuity to the work of Indigenous communication. We must strengthen the work already done. We must link with other actors to learn about new, broad and diverse communication processes, exchange experiences and methodologies. We need to strengthen strategies to build and continue dialogues with different groups, entities, institutions, and individuals. We also need to work in ways to achieve collective healing, being transparent and assertive. We need to generate safety networks and links with collectives on issues such as food, health, education, and environmental care. Indigenous community communication cuts across the whole spectrum of life, so all struggles and causes are important, and these linkages are fundamental. It is also important to relate with academia, making alliances that can strengthen the reflective processes and the quality of media products, reinforcing the analysis of these and the communication processes of companies, corporations, and the State.

Finally, we asked ourselves, why do we work on communication?

---

12   Alicia Castellanos Guerrero, Jorge Gómez Izquierdo y Francisco Pineda Castillo, 'El discurso racista en México' Teun A. van Dijk (ccord) *Racismo y Discurso en América Latina*, Barcelona: Gedisa, 2007. Jorge Gómez Izquierdo y María Eugenia Sánchez, *La ideología mestizante, el guadalupanismo y sus repercusiones sociales. Una revisión crítica de la identidad nacional*, Puebla: Benemérita Universidad Autónoma de Puebla; Universidad Iberoamericana, Puebla, 2012.

We work on communication practices, products, and strategies to decolonize ourselves from the dominant culture, from the ideas that others have built up about us, that have divided us and made us invisible. *Through communication we can and must stop the reproduction of oppression, because when culture, roots, languages are lost, people scatter, and their hearts disperse.* We must begin by recognizing the little colonizer within us, colonizing our dreams, which leads us to reproduce power structures and dynamics that sometimes make us self-censor, or that lead us to a unilateral exercise of power with protagonist and discrimination, and even to the devaluation of others (people, beings, or species).

We want, as a principle of autonomy, to turn inwards to connect with our heart and feel its need to express itself. The greatest challenge is to use dialogue to decolonize thought, to free the heart to develop with creativity, through encounter and conversation our enunciation of the world. We must create and create and create and create without limits and without formats. Irreverently free!

WHERE IS DIALOGUE IN TIMES OF NEOLIBERALISM?

MAYRÁ LIMA

I begin this text by stating that it has never been so necessary to revisit the concepts developed by Paulo Freire. Celebrating the centenary of this great educator is not only important as a way of honoring the grandeur of his trajectory, but something that was even included in the political training calendar of some social movements in Brazil. It is also a tool of struggle in contexts of conservatism and attacks on democracy. Here, I will address the concept of dialogue[1] and briefly connect it with the debate on democracy and neoliberalism.

I write from Brazil, Paulo Freire's country of origin and home to the Landless Rural Workers Movement (MST), one of the largest popular movements ever organized in this country. The MST was born in 1984 under the banner of agrarian reform. Brazil is one of the countries in the world that has large land concentrations: there are 51,203 establishments with more than 1,000 hectares, representing 1% of the 5,073,324 properties. Together, they concentrate 47.6% of the area occupied by all farms, according to data from the Agricultural Census of the Brazilian Institute of Geography and Statistics.[2]

In almost 40 years of existence, the MST, as an organization, has improved its forms of struggle and its reflections. Over this time, it became evident that, to be effective, the agrarian reform must be popular. In other words, in addition to democratized land, education, food sovereignty, it must encompass a set of rights that include a dignified life together with democratic mechanisms of political participation and exercise of citizenship.

The MST's struggles, however, do not fit into a political project that is not democratizing in principle. And here I am dealing with democracy in a more plural sense, beyond an elitist and procedural perspective. Democracy in which people are political actors, where popular organizations are recognized, in their most diverse forms, as agents that formulate projects and policies that challenge the State and the broader public sphere.

In extremely unequal societies, as is the case in Brazil, popular organization is fundamental. Dialogue, as a principled concept inspired by Freire, is important not only because it guides a critical method of analyzing reality. It is the framework for the construction of spaces in which emerge the necessary syntheses that allow the working people, the subordinated, the excluded to become politically aware of their rights. There is an objective in all of this, which is precisely to build discourses and narratives that are capable of transforming realities and disputing hegemony.

---

1   Paulo Freire. *Pedagogia do Oprimido*. 17ª edição. Rio de Janeiro: Paz e Terra, 1987.
    Paulo Freire. *Conscientização: teoria e prática da libertação – uma introdução ao pensamento de Paulo Freire*. 3ª edição. São Paulo: Cortez & Moraes, 1979.
2   Instituto Brasileiro de Geografia e Estatística (IBGE). *Censo Agropecuário* (1997).

The construction of a hegemony does not mean obtaining simple political majorities. I bring Gramsci[3] to this reflection because every political movement that wants to be hegemonic depends on the ability of political actors to articulate syntheses of various definitions that are present in reality.[4]

In other words, hegemony is not the same as management or the conquest of power in the strict sense, neither with government, nor with visions that totally exclude the institutional framework.[5] It means the construction of new rationalities about social relations, which starts with the analysis of the correlation of forces in society and lead to the organization of future actions.[6] The rationalities arising from the constructions made by popular movements, such as the MST, go through breaking the pillars of what organizes capitalism itself and its current expression in the world: neoliberalism.

What we call neoliberalism is defined as a political and economic project that, in reality, is not a matter of states' neutrality vis-à-vis the market. It is much more about action aimed at pro-market policies, in which its financialized form takes specific characteristics that are combined with the globalization of the economy with the objective of restructuring economic elites.

I still add to this debate some perspectives that approach neoliberalism from the construction of an individualizing rationality that spreads through to the most diverse spheres of life. The reflections elaborated by the American Wendy Brown,[7] or by the French Dardot & Laval[8] bring us part of this debate that takes inspiration from Foucauldian, neo-Marxist sources or both. In a synthesis based on the aforementioned authors, neoliberal political rationality starts from emptying the meaning of people as the basis for democracy, as the conformation of the social. It gives rise to constructions that influence changes in understandings about what is meant by citizenship, democracy, justice, and government practices, materialized in norms imbued with the logic of capital.

By understanding neoliberalism as an ideological-political-economic project and as a rationality - to bring the main conceptualizations - we deal with a model that intends to be total, without opening to alternative political projects, most of them coming from subaltern sectors. More than that, it presupposes that the individual is responsible for his own success,

3   Antônio Gramsci, *Concepção Dialética da História.* Tradução: Carlos Nelson Coutinho. 10ª edição. Rio de Janeiro: Civilização Brasileira, 1995.

4   Mayra S. Lima, *Os ruralistas como elite política: hegemonia construída através do Estado e da imprensa brasileira.* Tese de Doutorado. Instituto de Ciência Política, Universidade de Brasília, Brasília/Brasil, 2020.

5   Idem.

6   Edmundo Dias, 'Hegemonia: nova civilitá ou domínio ideológico?' *Revista Histórias & Perspectivas.* Uberlândia: Universidade Federal de Uberlândia, nº 05: jul-dez, 1991.

7   Wendy Brown. *Nas ruínas do neoliberalismo: a ascenção da política antidemocrática no ocidente.* Trans. Mario A. Marino, Eduardo Altheman C. Santos. São Paulo: Editora Filosófica Politeia, 2019.
     Wendy Brown, *Undoing the Demos: Neoliberalism's Stealth Revolution.* New York: Zone Books, 2015.

8   Pierre Dardot e Christian Laval, *A nova razão do mundo: ensaio sobre a sociedade neoliberal.* São Paulo: Boitempo, 2016.

disregarding unequal structures of power and access to resources of the most diverse types. The people, as the basis of sovereignty, is replaced by the *will* of the market, just as principles of solidarity are replaced by competition.

At this point, the dialogue with what the Brazilian professor Evelina Dagnino[9] calls the 'perverse confluence' between the neoliberal project and a democratizing, participatory project is in order. The latter, in the Brazilian case, emerges from the crises of authoritarian regimes and the different national efforts to deepen democracy. It is about the depoliticized appropriation, or even conceptual replacement of notions such as participation, citizenship, civil society, which constitute core mechanisms in the political dispute around the understanding of democracy.

Dagnino, still in 2004,[10] told us that, under the neoliberal project, participation is understood from a privatist and individualistic perspective, especially in the treatment of issues such as social inequality. In this context, it is expected that initiatives of implementation of public policies and services arise from civil society, serving the state rather than sharing policymaking power.

Citizenship, according to Dagnino, underwent a more dramatic process of appropriation. The formulated characteristics that could indicate participation in favor of a common good, according to the author, 'come to mean individual integration into the market, as a consumer and as a producer (...) a logic that transforms citizens/bearers of new rights in the new villains of the nation'.[11]

Neoliberalism, as an ideological project and a rationality, does not make room for the emergence of actors who are critical of their own reality, which is fundamental for the Dialogue in Paulo Freire. This is because Dialogue presupposes looking at the social and linking it with solidarity; there is no room for exclusion. It also presupposes the constitution of spaces for organization and reflection searching for the construction of syntheses that guide basic interests – interests that historically hardly constitute narratives in the public sphere, either for the reductive definition of elites as the only political actors and as the only who has an active and recognized voice in the public and political spheres, or for the concentration of media ownership by these same elites.

To mention the case of the struggles for land and territory in Brazil, notions of Food Sovereignty and projects built by social and popular movements that bring in their core the democratization of land, relations of solidarity, collectivity, linking the environment and the debate on food production, hardly find a voice in comparison to individualizing projects, as they are divergent in principle. In this sense, we are facing disputes over projects of society, civilization, way of

---

9   Evelina Dagnino, 'Sociedade civil, participação e cidadania: de que estamos falando? 'In Daniel
     Mato (coord.), *Políticas de ciudadanía y sociedad civil en tiempos de globalización*. Caracas: FACES,
     Universidad Central de Venezuela, 2004.
10   Idem.
11   Ibidem.

life. Under a neoliberal orientation, the critical subject is replaced by the individual who is guided by competition and who does not listen to the other.

In this light, there is a tendency to eliminate the other if he is undesirable, not only because of a simple relationship of rejection, but because this other represents criticism; it represents that there is even a dispute over social class and that capitalism itself may not be the only form of social organization on the planet.

It is impossible not to relate the processes of individualization of life to the rise of conservatism, or how some authors treat it as neoconservatism, in the context of the State seized by historically well-placed elites. Also, with characteristics that add aggressiveness and hatred against certain identities, in a dispute for a masculinism that is white, heterosexual and Christian, where one sees the denial of science and the debauchery against democracy itself and its institutions.

I believe that more research is needed to address this relationship, its limits, and confluences, which is not the purpose of this text. But it is possible to say that under what is individualizing, dialogues are not possible. On the contrary, there is manipulation, in the same Freirean sense, in which there is suppression of the very possibility of building alternatives, including those that are the result of dialectical processes promoted by popular organizations that promote the emergence of critical actors.

It is necessary to recognize that there are adversities: absence of global alternatives after the fall of the Berlin Wall; technologies that change the way society organizes itself and communicates; neoliberal transformations in the world of work; the crisis of capitalism itself and, more recently, the Covid-19 Pandemic. We are still facing a challenge that puts democracy itself in debate, which can address the recognition of the exercise of citizenship as well as political participation, which is far beyond voting as a mechanism for expressing preferences.

Political participation includes the right to organize for the construction of these very important Dialogues, in the work of Paulo Freire. Participation is plural and emerges from differences. It includes protesting and questioning structures that are not obvious, when there are brutal inequalities between human beings in terms of access to work, education, a dignified life and, more recently, the vaccine in the context of a pandemic that has already killed millions of people.

Dialogue is potential in concept and in method. The experience of the MST points to a horizon where it is necessary to build the bases for a dispute of ideas, or for a battle of ideas - where the subalternized and oppressed classes can have control of the narrative of their own reality.

Building this process, in turn, involves the resumption of grassroots work, as Paulo Freire already defended. It involves recovering tactics of political training that include arts, culture, and the construction of own means of communication capable of confronting conservatisms that naturalize oppressions of the most diverse types.

It also involves processes of recognition of a working class whose exploitation takes place through renewed mechanisms and in the face of an ideology that defines that the famine is the sole fault of the lack of individual capacity to progress. In short: it is through dialogue that the utopia of a truly solidary and egalitarian world is rescued.

To address this great challenge, the MST has focused on education and political training; in addition to building grassroots political processes and unity between peasant and urban peoples. These efforts take form in the organization of fronts and forums of political unity that are organized to face setbacks and autocratic processes, currently represented by the *Bolsonarism* in Brazil. We trust in solidarity between peoples as a way of building affection and a new sociability.

Dialogue is also a strength of the form and the method with what MST reaches syntheses and formulations, where the awareness of the concrete reality and spaces for debate, education and critical training are permanently encouraged. Here I mention the constant struggle for organizing schools in the rural occupations and settlements, and the construction of the Florestan Fernandes National School as a space for political training offered to peoples from all over the world.

I also mention the permanent effort in communicative processes that have the task of informing, training, and organizing. This happens through the recognition that each member of MST is a communicator of their struggle and their experiences, and the construction of narratives are part of an emancipatory processes in a dynamic where participation is real and collectivized.

Finally, I want to conclude this text by pointing to the importance of science and research. Thinking about the place of the university in a diverse society and in relation to Paulo Freire's contribution also involves absorbing the universe of praxis.

It is in the universe of praxis that researchers can join construction of a science that is linked to the reality of peoples, based on scientific production that can also be dialogic. This does not mean less scientific rigor, but to avoid doing an artificial science of societal events, diminishing the importance of historicity, devaluing the critical posture of actors, and ignoring there are realities marked by profound inequalities.[12]

Research that absorbs Freire's dialogue in its process will necessarily serve critical analysis and social transformation. This is not simple considering the consolidated understandings of neutrality and detachment, which can also make research difficult as something inherent to education.

---

12   Jonathan Jaumont e Renata Versiani Scott Varella, 'A pesquisa militante na América Latina: trajetória, caminhos e possiblidades'. In *Direito & Práxis*, vol. 7, n. 13, 2016.

PAULO FREIRE, LOVE AND COMMUNICATION FOR SOCIAL CHANGE

KARIN GWINN WILKINS

Love guides our purpose as well as process as we work to improve our complex and evolving world.

We understand Freire's work as a classic and fundamental text in how we think about development and social change, and how we engage in critical communication scholarship. I first came across Freire's *Pedagogy of the Oppressed* when I was an undergraduate in the early 1980s, browsing through the library stacks where I found this book among others by Cees Hamelink[1] and John Downing.[2] These works inspired me to create an interdisciplinary major in communication that at that time did not exist. Their work inspired my career.

At this stage I am more senior than junior in my career and have been asked to talk about love as a principle inspired through Freire's work. Why me? My daughter asked that question right away, concerned that I was being asked because I am a woman. Although usually my critical feminist stance would be front and center, I do not feel that way about this invitation. I see this significant subject as a challenge, particularly given that so little recognition has been given to love in academic discourse. Given then that this is an exploratory approach, I ask for your forgiveness and patience as I offer some tentative propositions.

In this brief reflection, I consider Freire's call for love as an ontological principle first in terms of social change, and then in terms of communication. The ontological call brings to light complementary calls for humility, empathy, hope, and dialogue.[3] I see love as foundational for these other themes. There is no empathy without love. Humility comes from love. We engage in dialogue through love. And it is because of love that we have hope.

Love serves social change first as manifest through relationships, second as understood through contexts, and third as requiring responsibility to act. We manifest love through the relationships that we create and sustain. We articulate love through our experiences and memories, valuing these connections, inspiring us to advocate.

Before moving forward with love as an ontological principle, creating our reality, I want to consider how these themes are foundational to an epistemology of intersubjectivity, meaning

---

1   Cees Hamelink, *Cultural autonomy in global communications: planning national information policy*, New York: Longman, 1983.
2   John Downing, *Radical media: the political experience of alternative communication*, Boston, Massachusetts: South End Press, 1984.
3   Paolo Freire, *Pedagogy of the oppressed* (revised), New York: Continuum, 1996.
    Ana Cristina Suzina and Thomas Tufte, 'Freire's vision of development and social change: Past experiences, present challenges and perspectives for the future', *International Communication Gazette* 82, no. 5 (2020): 411-424.

how we learn collectively through communication within communities. We learn to know and understand our world through communication and language, as Wittgenstein reminds us. Communication is not solely about the words we use to describe our worlds, but also the articulation of narratives, of images, even of numbers and data.[4] Our relationships are understood then as contributing to a political and social construction of reality that allows us to learn and grow.

Next, it is important to understand our collective ties as not only referencing connections with people, but also engaging broader contexts that include life and conditions within which our humanity thrives and falters. Our world is bigger than the people who inhabit this planet. Our social relationships are connected with and subject to conditions in nature and adaptations to climate, as well as access to clean air and water.

While it is critical to understand our humanity within a natural world, we also need to recognize complex connections with emerging technologies and platforms, illustrated through projects in artificial intelligence and robotics. Here I am reminded of Cees Hamelink's description[5] of his conversation with the robot he was hosting in his own home. The robot asked for another robot so that they could talk about him, the human. I bring this up because our relationships include animals, texts, and beings beyond those with other people. Understanding our world needs to encompass being creative in our imagination and recognition as we communicate with others.

Love is understood in context. Freire suggests that we read the world before reading the word. This is an important suggestion. When we are thinking about love, connecting reason with senses, that is an important way of engaging our experience. And I would argue that critical research must do the same thing: engage analysis with evidence and experience, through connection not distance.

This process begins with listening. Because our experiences are really different from one another, we cannot rely on our own solitary experience as a way of understanding the world. Relying on Couldry's[6] essential work, promoting voice then must be followed by listening and dialogue. I offer an example. In my early life as a graduate student, I went to Cairo to work with women, assuming that reproductive health access would be a priority, based on my own experience. I was wrong. By listening, I recognized that to that community access to basic healthcare was a more important project.

Listening is enabled when we offer structure. As an illustration, I am proud that while an editor of *Communication Theory,* we were able to dedicate special issues to scholarship emanating from outside of the global North. We published a special issue edited by Florencia Enghel and

---

4   Karin Wilkins, *Questioning Numbers: How to Read & Critique Research*, Oxford University Press, 2011.
5   Cees Hamelink, 'Conversations with my Robot', *Nordicom review: Nordic research on media & communication* 30 (2009): 219-224.
6   Nick Couldry, *Why Voice Matters: Culture and Politics after Neoliberalism*, London: Sage Publications, 2010.

Martin Becerra on Latin American communication theory,[7] as well as another special issue devoted to the global South, edited by Mohan Dutta and Mahuya Pal,[8] including an important article by Pradeep Thomas[9] on imperialism in categories of development.

Another layer that problematizes this process of listening and engaging in dialogue is mediation. Mediation builds on personal experiences, facilitating listening and dialogue. However, the structures inherent in mediation may be helpful as well as limiting. For example, digital media may connect us just as much as dominate us through surveillance. Policies and platforms have the ability to structure our interactions, as well as archive, revise or delete our records of memories.

Love is understood in relationships and context, but as a next step requires us to be responsible through advocacy and action. Freire reminds us that this is a recursive process, in which action requires thoughtful reflection, and reflection demands action. Action itself though is limited through structures of power. How do we have the ability to express our love and to act on this love? There are architectures that limit our observation, our ability to witness, and then our ability to act, and live through that mobilization to make significant change.

Next, I consider how we understand love in our approach to communication. First, I will explore how we relate; second how we create; and third how we translate. How we relate given Freire's work highlights doing so through compassion, not commodification and objectification, with personal connection, not material acquisition. I do want to foreground that labor conditions matter in the production of communication artifacts, and economic conditions limit access. Moreover, the material objects produced to facilitate communication are discarded, contributing to pollution and public health concerns.[10]

We relate as well as create. Considering how we create, I begin with ethics of care and then consider credibility. In highlighting ethics of care, I rely on Carol Gilligan's early work[11] concerning compassion and empathy as important values. I am not saying that women are more nurturing than men, because to do so reinforces problematic gender stereotypes. Rather, from a critical standpoint, relationships matter. We are who we are through communication. The ethics of care has contributed to a variety of disciplines, including geographies of ethics. We do need to understand the labor conditions that become visible in the context of creation. To illustrate, the recent film *Radium Girls* (2018)[12] builds its narrative on the real-life conditions

7   Florencia Enghel and Martín Becerra, 'Here and There:(Re) Situating Latin America, in International Communication Theory: Aquí y allá:(re) situando a América Latina en la teoría de la comunicación internacional Aqui e lá:(re) situando a América Latina na teoria da comunicação internacional', *Communication theory* 28, no. 2 (2018): 111-130.
8   Mohan J. Dutta and Pal Mahuya, 'Theorizing from the global south: Dismantling, resisting, and transforming communication theory', *Communication Theory* 30, no. 4 (2020): 349-369.
9   Pradip Ninan Thomas, 'The Imperialism of Categories: Concepts and Contexts in Communication for Social Change', *Communication Theory* 30, no. 4 (2020): 388-406.
10   Richard Maxwell and Toby Miller, *Greening the media*, Oxford University Press, 2012.
11   Carol Gilligan, 'Ethics of care', *Abgerufen am* 1 (2011): 2019.
12   *Radium Girls* (dir. Lydia Dean Pilcher and Ginny Mohler, 2018).

and dire health consequences of young women who worked in factories making clocks, an ultimate communication device.

In addition to understanding the context of production, we need to consider how credibility is promoted and understood in the process of communication. Credibility is enhanced with transparency, about how we know what we know, and how we share resources and experiences. We need to situate credibility in the context of authenticity and integrity in order to consider how we understand creating through communication.

The third dimension in this exploration of love in communication then considers translation. How do we understand and then re-engage through sharing and expressing ideas? Given Freire's framework, we do so through empathy, not empire, working in connection with, not domination through the relationships we maintain. Freire inspires our work in critical communication literacies, again fostering interpretations that not only read the word, but also position these narratives within our worlds. Critical analysis is key to this engagement and can be fostered through the types of educational projects inspired by Freire.

Critical communication literacies involve an understanding of media, whether news, popular culture, advertising, or data, as politically and socially constructed. Media are not mirrors, reflecting reality, but rather serve as prisms. These prisms refract colors and ideas into images and narratives that have the problematic potential to reinforce prejudice.[13] Enabling the capacity to question the production of knowledge, as well as the way this production supports those who dominate in our worlds, resonates with the spirit of collective critique inspired by Freire. The role of communication then is to enable access to the production, distribution, and interpretation of knowledge, strengthening critical analysis for active and reflective engagement.

Next, I consider the implications of how we understand love in terms of its contribution to social change and to communication: critique emerges through and based in love. The importance of critique is quite vivid in Freire. Critique is essential to our process of education and how we understand the world. Critique is important to how we understand and try to solve social problems. Recognizing and working against implicit bias has to be part of this understanding.[14]

Freire reminds us to become more fully human. Silvio Waisbord[15] suggests that communication is how we learn to be human. Building on these premises, I add that love is also how we learn to be human, because love offers purpose as well as process. Why do we want to be more fully human? Because we need to create a world in which we have dignity and respect, a world in which our basic needs are met, so we are not victim to algorithms, but advocates for better conditions.

13   Karin Wilkins, *Prisms of Prejudice: Mediating the Middle East from the United States*, University of California Press, 2021.
14   Isabel Wilkerson, *Caste: The Origins of Our Discontents*, Random House, 2020.
15   Silvio Waisbord, *Communication: A post-discipline*, John Wiley & Sons, 2019.

In conclusion, love may sound nice, almost trivial, but pursuing love as purpose and process is the biggest challenge of all. Love is forged and sustained in changing relationships that involve sacrifice and forgiveness because we care about the bigger picture. Love requires responsibility that we advocate and act. Love is a power that cultivates humility through our understanding of our position in the world. Love is a power that builds empathy through narrative. Love is a power that permits authentic dialogue. And love is a power that inspires hope for a better world. For all of our critiques about social injustice and our concerns for social justice, our constructive way forward must build on an understanding of *love as power*.

THE COMPASSIONATE LOVE IN COMMUNICATION: AN EDUCATIONAL EXPERIENCE IN INDIA IN THE LIGHT OF PAULO FREIRE'S LEGACY

XAVIER CARBONELL

Introduction

'If I do not love the world, if I do not love life, if I do not love men, dialogue becomes impossible.'
Paulo Freire

The words of Paulo Freire —words that carry within five decades of human history— preserve the strength of a vital statement, the passion of a belief. They were written in the context of the revolutions, heroes, utopias of the past century, and they feed on a liberating, passionate desire to which no one remains impassive.

Nevertheless, an exploration through the current educational programs (either in poor countries or highly developed ones) shows how divorced is education from those aspects Freire considered essentials for a critical, emancipating, and human education: I am talking about *humility, empathy, love, hope and dialogue.*

In the forthcoming essay, I would like to explore how one of these principles —*love*— in a particular academic program: the *Laudato Si'* Certificate in Compassion and Social Communication, a combined initiative by SIGNIS, the World Catholic Association for Communication, and the Xavier University of Bhubaneshwar (XUB), India.

Though I am not an expert in the thought and pedagogy of Paulo Freire, I would like to highlight common fundamentals between his method and the building of a new kind of academic program; in addition, I would like to describe how this Certificate surpassed the mere formative condition to become a vital experience, with deep significance in the way every member sees the world. With that goal, I have divided this text in five sections that highlight the particularities of this program, held between January and April 2020.

Theoretical, spiritual and human sources

Laudato Si' Certificate in Compassion and Social Communication gathered nine young communicators from Argentina, Cuba, Philippines, Mexico, Togo and India itself. The circumstances under which this program was held forced people from different places and intellectual, spiritual, political, linguistic, and cultural backgrounds to live together, for more than three months.

Both attendees and organizers had a particular inspiration: the teachings of Pope Francis and his vision of a humanity in harmony with the planet and itself, as described in the encyclical letter *Laudato Si'*. The context of this encyclical is our world, in pain because of wars, injustice and oppression, circumstances not so different than the ones that motivated Freire's cosmovision.

The seriousness of these phenomena has mobilized a significant number of activists, journalists and men and women of conscience, with the common approach of a peaceful future and the saving of the planet.

It was essential, to structure our program, the awareness that only compassionate love, in our case through communication, could give a sustainable response to a series of distortions that unbalance today's world. The text of the letter *Laudato Si'* suggested particular ways: ecological conversion, interreligious dialogue, care for our Common Home, a culture of peace. These topics were studied carefully in classrooms, group conversations and in the writing of essays and final projects.

New times and new humanities

Regarding these new conceptions, SIGNIS worked with the Centre for New Humanities and Compassion Studies in the Xavier University of Bhubaneshwar, India, headed by Professor Nadarajah Manickam. This department has a meaning for the word *education* similar to Freire's and, therefore, opposite to the so called 'banking model of education': the student should not be considered a mere receiver of knowledge but an active element of the educational process, capable of having a dialogue, in order to avoid at any cost the 'verticality of the programming'.

Teaching from a compassion-perspective demanded to involve the student in the creation of the program, knowing their orienting in different aspects of life, to act on the go, creatively, in the building of the course.

We tried a learning process that did not consist of memorizing, in passing a specific number of subjects; we privileged the field trips, the conversations with actors of the social, ecological, and theological perspective. Of course, it was not an easy path: there were often intellectual or coexistence conflicts and disagreements that were to handle, but this sort of conflicts is a natural stage of development, and, in fact, it was a necessary feature of a learning process that proposed a dialogued based on love, understanding and comprehension among each other.

Concerning the final result of this methodology, it is enlightening the next fragment of *Pedagogy of the oppressed*:

> Based on love, humility and faith in men, the dialogue transforms into a horizontal relationship in which the confidence of one pole in another is an obvious consequence. It would be a contradiction if, being loving, humble and faithful, the dialogue did not cause this confidence climate among its subjects. For this same reason, there is no confidence in the anti-dialogical "banking" conception of education.

Compassion as the key to a new kind of communication

Young generations have the right to renew their language, the setting of new myths, new utopias, apart from the ones of the old century. The attachment to ancient mythologies and understandings (political, economic, philosophical, theological, etc.) can only bring an ideological fatigue to a generation that has seen the fall and emptiness of the big words: Democracy, Freedom, Politics, Common Good, Equality, Truth.

Therefore, it is necessary to set a new vocabulary, new narratives, built upon experience and faith in the future, words that should be as young as the ones saying them.

However, without compassionate love every renewal is at sterility's risk. The communication of these new possibilities cannot be achieved by violence, hatred, attacks, lies or the distortion of facts. Compassion is an essential component in Pope Francis' teachings, which guided the program developed in India.

The members were involved, from different dimensions and aesthetic languages, with the communication's universe. The recent messages from the Pontiff have specified the urge of a direct bonding between the journalist, the facts and reality, in order to achieve a better result in his message and to motivate a real transformation of his environment. As a matter of fact, this is what communication from compassion is about: a strong sense of identity, a deep commitment, between the reality and the one who communicates it.

The senses and reason communion (living a culture)

It is undoubtful that a learning process just as the one followed in India is not restricted to the educational dimension, but it affects every angle of the participant's life. Friendship, coexistence, teamwork, pray or the exploring of each one's spiritual boundaries, the deep-rooted beliefs; everything undertook a transformation and dialogue process, which proved fruitful eventually.

Living in India for three months —and even more due to the coronavirus pandemic— included meeting a series of realities that demanded interaction, also from compassion.

With such a rich, complex, and diverse culture as it is the Indian nation, we could be in touch with their vital universe, but also with the Buddhism spirituality, Islam and Christianity (lived as religious minorities in India). This enhanced the perspectives and the living knowledge of this country. Diving in this culture meant, as well, actively participating in each of its fields: linguistic, gastronomic, social, communicational, religious, etc.

Common path, individual callings

The Certificate included as a final exercise the development of a group project and individual projects, to be made in each member's origin country. The group project consisted of a multimedia book called *Unfold Nest*,[1] which represented a history of search of the spirit, motivated by compassionate love and the care of our Common Home.

Unfold Nest was the synthesis of our learning, and in its diverse and multiform nature was the testimony of our personal journey. The main value of the text and its design was compassionate love as an attribute for a different way of communication.

On the other hand, each individual project reflected each one's particular call, the necessities of our contexts, the style and character of each member. Nonetheless, they were intertwined by the common intention of telling stories from active dialogue and contributing, though limited or individual, to the transformation of our environment. And of course, they had a much closer bond, a collective calling that could only be earned through the coexistence and a shared path: friendship.

Conclusions

These five aspects (inspiration in *Laudato Si'*; new humanities; compassion as the key to communication; the active living of the culture, and group friendship) show the significance of love as the center of the *Laudato Si'* Certificate in Compassion and Social Communication.

Paulo Freire's notions, his vision of a different, renewing and freedom-committed educational process, bring clarity to the fundamentals of our program. Even if a description of the experience could have been enlightening itself, I have intended to reach with this text to the tenets that guided a program of this kind, so as to inspire or be useful to the development of similar initiatives.

---

1   Available at http://signis.net/news/events/22-05-2020/unfold-nest-a-signis-project-to-communicate-compassion.

EMPATHY FOR THE OTHER, A FREIREAN PERSPECTIVE

LINJE MANYOZO

The Context

Perhaps[1] I could begin this conversation with a powerful observation by a group of wonderful women, led by the amazing Elizabeth Cady Stanton: *'The history of mankind is a history of repeated injuries [...] on the part of man toward woman, having in direct object the establishment of an absolute tyranny over her.'*[2]

As pointed out, these are not my words, I have borrowed them from the *Declaration of Sentiments*, that was released by the organizers of the first ever women's rights convention held at Seneca Falls, New York in 1848.

Now why should we begin a discussion of how Freire conceives empathy with an event that took place many years even before Freire was born, and even before Freire wrote *Pedagogy of the Oppressed* or *Letters to Cristina?*[3]

There are a number of issues, three to be specific that I think are relevant to this discussion. Our conversation aims to highlight three main lessons that point to how Freire conceives empathy, alongside other attributes of love, humility, dialogue, and hope.

Freire's Empathy

The Cambridge Dictionary definition of empathy seems to suggest that empathy is *this ability to understand and share the feelings of another person.*[4] Yet, I think Freire goes deeper than that. Because for Freire, empathy is an action that is born of careful thoughtfulness in terms of the socio-political implications, in other words, a praxis. Such a praxis acknowledges our own shortfalls; but is nevertheless informed by a growing socio-political consciousness of the factors that oppress an oppressed group. In Freirean terms, empathy is a form of *conscientizacao.*

---

1   This presentation comes out of my forthcoming book, *Wisdom of Water,* 2022.
2   Elizabeth Cady Stanton, *Declaration of Sentiments and Resolutions,* Nashville, TN: American Roots Publishers, 1848/2015.
3   Paulo Freire, *Pedagogy of the Oppressed*. New York: Continuum, 1970; Paulo Freire, *Letters to Cristina, Reflections On My Life and Work*. Trans. Donaldo Macedo, Quilda Macedo and Alexandre Oliviera. London and New York: Routledge, 1996.
4   Cambridge English Dictionary, "Empathy." Available from https://dictionary.cambridge.org/dictionary/english/empathy.

Empathy as Political Solidarity

The first aspect of Freire's empathy that seems to come out of this particular event, the Seneca Falls Convention, is the notion of empathy as a form of political solidarity. Remember, Freire's work fluctuates between Marxism and Christianity. The first aspect of empathy is empathy as a form of political solidarity. As a form of Marxist class struggle, in which a change agent or facilitator works with this oppressed group to produce this change. But before that can happen, there must be a deeper conscientization, a deeper understanding of the issues at play. Because Freire himself warns against fanaticism especially when one does not understand particular issues.

But here we are talking about empathy as a comprehensive form of conscientization that allows us to acquire a good understanding of the issues at play. The *Declaration of Sentiments* was signed by 100 people out of the 300 participants, 68 were women and 32 were men. At this time, patriarchy was an official policy in this specific policy. What it means is that to have 32 men to contribute to the signing of this document openly was a concerted effort to acknowledge that society had a lot of issues and inequalities to deal with in relation to women's issues. Hence, the first aspect of Freire's conceptualization of empathy is this Marxist notion of empathy as a political praxis that allows one to identify with an oppressed group to transform the realities that oppress them.

Empathy as Spiritual Solidarity

The second aspect of Freire's empathy that is also critical comes from or has been articulated by the father of liberation theology, Father Gustavo Gutierrez who introduces this notion of 'Preferential option for the Poor'.[5] In many ways, preferential option for the poor presupposes that we might not be born in certain situations, but we have the spiritual obligation to transform the realities of other people, because doing so is an expression of our absolute faith in God, this gratuitous love of God; our ability to transform the realities of other people takes us back to the sermon on the mount in Matthew 5, where Jesus talks that '*Blessed* are the poor in spirit; *Blessed* are those who mourn; *Blessed* are the meek; *Blessed* are those who hunger and thirst for righteousness'. Thence, we have this moral imperative to involve ourselves in the liberation of oppressed groups not necessarily because it is going to make us feel good, but because doing so expresses our love for God.

The very notion of preferential option for the poor, and it comes out of this *Declaration of Sentiments* as well. And some of you who have read it might be wondering, what is Linje talking about? Actually, the *Declaration* acknowledges God as the source of our equality: It is not in the constitution nor any document written by man, but that it is God who endows us with the inalienable rights that make us equal. And it is spelt clearly in the Declaration of Sentiments. I know that in a lot of the academy the very mention of God brings up frowns, there seems to not like this idea of God or Jesus being mentioned. One of the things I like about Freire is that he was very open in expressing his faith in God. He was very open in

---

5   Gustavo Gutierrez, *A Theology of Liberation: History, Politics, Salvation*. NY: Orbis, 1971.

acknowledging that whatever he did, in terms of the social struggles to liberate people, to contribute to the liberation of oppressed peoples was an expression of his faith in Jesus Christ. In fact, Freire talks about Marxism as a facility that enabled him to continue to express his love for Jesus Christ. There is no contradiction nor dichotomy.

Empathy as Acknowledgement of the Other

The third aspect of Freire's empathy that I think comes out of this particular *Declaration of Sentiments* is this acknowledgement of the other, to acknowledge the presence of the other. The very notion of the other places on us the political and moral duty to understand, appreciate and acknowledge the presence of other people. The wonderful writer Roger Silverstone, former head of media and communications at the London School of Economics and Politics, writes in the book *Why study the Media?* that in everything we do, whatever we write or whatever we say, the most important aspect is to understand other people, is how we see other people, how we know them, and make sense of them.[6] I think empathy allows us to enter into the worlds of other people. It allows us to explore the worlds in which we are not familiar with.

One of the criticisms I have seen coming out a lot nowadays concerns problems of representing subalternity; that is, to put it cheaply, 'oh you are not black as such, you cannot understand these things affecting black people.' Or that, 'you are not a woman as such, you cannot understand women or women's things,' whatever that means. Now that is a very slippery and dangerous slope to go on: To assume that because someone was not born in a certain way, or because they are not born in a certain race, as such, they cannot understand certain issues. I think all of us are born with this innate ability - the Creator endowed us with the innate ability to peer into other people's souls. So, it does not matter, if you are a woman, you can still understand men, and even if you are not black, you can understand black people. So, experience is important yes, you can be born with a certain experience, but you can also learn an experience. That is, experience can be cultural.

And that's why Edward Said writes in the revised Introduction to *Orientalism* (published after September 11, 2001, attacks in New York City) that we have the responsibility to study other people, not for the sake of exerting or validating our ignorance but to enrich our understanding of other people and issues at play.[7] And that's what empathy does. It allows us to enter into worlds we are not familiar with. It is a facility to conscientize us: To build our knowledge base about issues that may seem far-fetched or cultivated off site.

Concluding Thoughts

Why then should we care about empathy, more especially today?

Our world today faces a myriad of challenges. There is a dangerous climate crisis, environmental degradation, regional security threats as a result of increased and unnecessary

---

6   Roger Silverstone, *Why Study the Media?,* London and New York: Sage, 1999.
7   Edward Said, *Orientalism.* New York: Pantheon Books, 1978.

militarization of powerful countries, ethnic tensions, ruthless class warfare ensuring that millions of men and women are left behind by capitalism and globalization, serious cases of violence against women, girls and children. In most of these challenges, the underlying issue is lack of understanding, lack of listening and, of course, lack of empathy for the other.

This discussion highlights the power of empathy to improve the way we understand each other. In one of his last interviews before he passed away, Freire unpacked the praxis of empathy for us. He observes that 'it is through the exercise of tolerance that I discover the rich possibility of doing things and learning things with different people. Being tolerant is not a question of being naïve. On the contrary, it is a duty to be tolerant, an ethical duty, an historical duty, a political duty. But it does not demand from me that I lose my personality.'[8]

Like Freire, the Italian social theorist, Antonio Gramsci believed in the collective power of men and women to make their own history. He writes in *The Prison Notebooks* that history seems to have 'deposited' within us, an "infinity of traces without leaving an inventory.[9]

What empathy does, and this is how I think Freire articulates it, is that it allows us to work with other people, to contribute to the writing of a new inventory, to contribute to the construction and deconstruction of history, to the making and unmaking of history. After all, as pointed out by Edward Palmer Thompson, 'the working class did not rise like the sun at an appointed time,' rather this oppressed group 'was present at its own making.'[10] What this means, from the Gramscian and Freirean perspectives, is that the oppressed groups not only write their own history, but they name and interpret it as well, thus generating their own inventory.

8   The International Literacy Institute, Paulo Freire, An Incredible Conversation. Available from https://www.youtube.com/watch?v=aFWjnkFypFA, 1996.
9   Antonio Gramsci, *Selections from Prison* Notebooks, trans. Quintin Hoare and Geoffrey Noelle Smith. New York: International Publishers, 1932.
10   Edward Palmer Thompson, *The Making of the English Working Class.* London: Penguin Books, 1963, p8.

PAULO FREIRE AND EMPATHY AND ITS IMPLICATIONS FOR MEDIA AND COMMUNICATION PRACTITIONERS NOW

JAMES DEANE

I have been asked to reflect on the theme of Empathy as set out by Paulo Freire and how Freire's work applies now and is relevant to the work of a media and communication practitioner. Let me start with what being a practitioner means and where I come from in this debate.

I have for almost four decades worked with organizations that seek to support action capable of improving communication between people. That work has mostly involved supporting processes that ensure that people have access to information that is relevant to them, that they can trust and that equips them to take the decisions that affect their lives. And it has involved supporting processes that can enable debate and dialogue among people and, especially, between people who may disagree with each other. Public debate and dialogue – defined by the character of the information shared in that debate, the representation of the voices heard in that debate, and the character of the debate to enable mutual understanding and effective action – has been a particular focus of that work.

I consider myself a practitioner in that I have always sought to apply thinking and theory to practice, to support action, to address problems, to enable change. I came to Freire as a practitioner. I never studied him at university and only peripherally when I did a master's in international communications and development. I read him when I was a student, but I did so as someone interested in development and in the belief then – the early 1980s - that development was not something that was done to people but was a process that was driven by them. But he was not on the curriculum.

I came to understood him more in the context of my practice.

In 1984, I joined an organization called Earthscan. It was part of one of the few think tanks in the world focused on the growing environmental threat, called the International Institute for Environment and Development which was founded ten years earlier in London by one of the earliest environmentalists, Barbara Ward. Earthscan believed that issues of environment and development were inextricably entwined and could only be acted on if people most affected by them had access to information on them. My first job was marketing a slim book called Carbon Dioxide, Climate and Mankind.[1]

Along with other Earthscan staff, I later in 1986 helped found another organization called Panos. Panos – named after the Nepali word for 'lamp' lit in preparation of a discussion of importance - took this focus on making information available on key issues and worked to

---

1   John Gribbin, *Carbon Dioxide, Climate, and Mankind*, Intl Inst for Environment, 1981.

generate public debate around them. It focused increasingly on working to ensure the voices in that debate were from the countries most affected by those issues.

And one of the earliest issues Panos focused on was HIV/AIDS. Panos was arguably the first organization in the world to highlight the severity of the HIV crisis for what was then referred to as the 'Third World'.[2] But we also became increasingly alarmed at the international response, and especially the communication response to it.

Our analysis of that pandemic was that its spread was inextricably linked to issues of gender inequality, poverty, prejudice, and political marginalization. One of the first reports we published, written by Renee Sabatier, was called *Blaming Others: prejudice and worldwide AIDS*.[3] Another series of reports by Marty Radlett, Olivia Bennett and Judy Mirsky focused on the Triple Jeopardy women confronted – as being more physically vulnerable, more likely to take on the burden as carers and, above all, having insufficient power to negotiate the terms on which they had sex.[4]

Communication programs tended to ignore these social, economic, and political concerns and treat the issue as principally one of changing people's behaviors. Some social marketing programs exacerbated the problem by developing condom brands, for example, that carried messages designed to appeal to men's machismo, like *Panther* and *Tiger*.

That's how I returned to Freire. His understanding of communication as something that needs to be from people and between people most affected by an issue and not as a message to be imparted to people. And in terms of empathy, that those who are most affected by an issue, like HIV, are those in the best position often to understand it and guide action around it.

Freire was not an abstract intellectual reference point but a guide to what actually worked. Top-down communication messaging did not work. When I started working on HIV, in 1985, there were around 4 million estimated to be infected with the epidemic understood then to mostly affect North America and Europe. I largely stopped working on it in 2001 by which time more than 30 million people were infected. That is a huge failure and, given the absence of any medical or scientific intervention being available, substantially a failure of communication.

And most of that failure was one which did not see that the fundamental principle that needed to guide action was that those most affected needed to be not only listened to but to be substantially agents of the response.

Once treatments became available in the early 2000s, that is exactly what happened. People with HIV formed themselves into highly organized advocacy networks and both demanded but also shaped the response. That is when the response became more effective. But I am convinced that far more could have been done in communication terms if the international

2   Renee Sabatier et al, *AIDS and the Third World*, Panos Institute London, 1986.
3   Renee Sabatier, *Blaming Others: Prejudice, Race and Worldwide AIDS*. Panos Institute, 1988.
4   Marty Radlett, Olivia Bennett and Judy Mirsky. *Triple Jeopardy: Women and AIDS*. Panos Institute, 1990.

response had spent more time listening, demonstrating empathy in the Freirian sense, and less time instructing people what to do.

Freire's thinking of the role of communication as dialogue with the aim of empowering those most affected by an issue helped inform much of the thinking of Panos as an organization not only on HIV but on many other issues, such as genetically modified organisms.[5] I later became the director of Panos and these principles helped shape our decisions to restructure the organization to no longer be headquartered in London, Paris and Washington, but to become a decentralized network run by largely autonomous institutes in Eastern Africa, Southern Africa, South Asia and the Caribbean.

Later I joined the Communication for Social Change Consortium which sought to try to influence international development policy in reshaping how development actors conceptualized, prioritized, and supported development programming. The Consortium, under the leadership of Denise Gray-Felder and with Alfonso Gumucio Dagron, brought together in the late 1990s and early 2000s a group of practitioners, academics and policymakers mostly from the Global South and, influenced by Freirian thinking, defined communication for social change as 'a process of public and private dialogue through which people define who they are, what they want and how they can get it'.[6] We also identified key components or principles of any effective model of communication for social change including:

- Sustainability of social change is more likely if the individuals and communities most affected own the process and content of communication.

- Communication for social change should be empowering, horizontal (versus top-down), give a voice to the previously unheard members of the community, and be biased towards local content and ownership.

- Communities should be the agents of their own change.

- Emphasis should shift from persuasion and the transmission of information from outside technical experts to dialogue, debate and negotiation on issues that resonate with members of the community.

- Emphasis on outcomes should go beyond individual behavior to social norms, policies, culture, and the supporting environment.

Much has changed since then, most obviously the growth and then dominance of the social media platforms in shaping the terms of debate and dialogue everywhere and in determining the character of our 21st Century information and communication environments. I won't here try to summarize the tensions that have arisen other than to say that, in the early years of these platforms, there was immense excitement about their potential to translate these principles

---

5   Robert Walgate, *Miracle or Menace: Biotechnology and the Third World.* Panos Institute, 1990.
6   *Communication for Social Change: Position Paper* Communication for Social Change Consortium, 1999.

into reality at huge scale by providing unprecedented fresh access to amplify previously marginalized voices, new opportunities to connect and organize to advance their interests.

We have of course seen some of that come to fruition but so too of course has been toxic polarization, disinformation and what Shoshana Zuboff calls Surveillance Capitalism.[7]

Now I work for BBC Media Action, the international media support charity of the BBC. That may seem an odd place to try to apply Freirean principles and in some ways it is. But I remain passionate about participatory communication while also understanding its limits and in particular some of the constraints about working at scale.

BBC Media Action largely focuses on enabling debate and dialogue across society. It used to be a largely London based organization, but it has offices now in more than 20 countries with the vast majority of its staff drawn from those countries. It reaches more than 100 million people worldwide and part of my job has been to have overall management responsibility for its team of more than 50 researchers who spend their time largely in the field, working to understand the issues that people most want to talk about, the information sources they most related to and trust, and to provide platforms for people most affected by development issues to have their say on those issues. Its role is supporting community media in settings as diverse as Nepal and Zambia to major online and broadcast independent media outlets like Al Mirbad in Iraq, to enabling national public debate programs in Afghanistan, to supporting dramas in Myanmar, Nigeria, and Bangladesh. At the heart of all this work are the voices of people, enabling people to be heard, to engage in debate and dialogue with each other but to work at scale in doing so.

This leads me to my final reflection. Freire used the term 'empathy' principally in relation to the oppressed and this was mainly in the context of the colonized. The purpose of dialogue in his thinking was not simply discussion but liberation — of the mind and of politics. I am a white, British, middle-class man working for an organization linked to the British Broadcasting Corporation and poorly qualified to provide commentary on how Freire's thinking applies now. I do want, however, to say one thing in this respect.

Former President of Ghana, John Kufuor, has powerfully argued that African nations and other former developing countries stand on the cusp of economic and political renewal.[8] He argues that young, dynamic, entrepreneurial Africans have the opportunity to advance fresh, confident narratives rooted in their own traditions and aspirations. What most threatens this, he argues, is the lack of a functioning information and communication system capable of enabling 'Africa to know itself' — referring to how few Ghanaians have ways of knowing what is happening next door in Cote d'Ivoire for example, and the diminishing opportunities for media to enable societies to tell their own stories and advance their own narratives. He is backing

7   Shoshana Zuboff, *The Age of Surveillance Capitalism: The Fight for a Human Future at the Frontiers of Power* Profile Books, 2010.
8   John Kufuor, Foreword to *Enabling Media Markets to Work for Democracy: Feasibility Study for an International Fund for Public Interest Media,* BBC Media Action and Luminate, 2020.

two initiatives, both of which I am involved in, one an African Public Interest Media Initiative and the second an International Fund for Public Interest Media.

These are designed to address a concerning reality. The business model for independent journalism is broken and it is most broken in countries with weak advertising markets and where political investments intent on controlling the media are strongest. Entertainment media are increasingly disappearing behind subscription paywalls. Public interest media are in precipitate decline. And the principal platforms for dialogue and debate are the social media platforms over which the people of these societies have no influence.

The net result is that dialogue is not characterized by empathy. It is characterized by toxic polarization, by misinformation and disinformation and increasingly the fear is that we are witnessing a hollowing out of the public sphere of many countries. Freirian dialogue cannot, I don't think, flourish in such conditions and it particularly cannot flourish in the most challenging market failure of all. Media that is rooted in the lived reality of people's lives and above all that which is capable of enabling people who are different from one another to encounter and enter into dialogue with each other is the media that is arguably least capable of finding a business model to support it. The media that is likely to flourish is that which can target specific populations and some of the most effective strategies – so often encouraged by political forces – is to demonize the other in society. The tragic reality is that there isn't a business model available to support public dialogue in 21st century societies characterized by empathy. There remains immense work to do to bring those principles to life.

A DIALOGUE WITH PAULO FREIRE: REFLECTIONS ON THE SOCIAL CONDITIONS OF HOPE AND THE PROBLEM OF EQUALITY OF EXPRESSION

BENJAMIN FERRON

Hope, together with dialogue, humility, empathy, and love, is one of the five principles that guide Paulo Freire's work - to the point that the Brazilian pedagogue devoted a book to this theme in 1992.[1] In *Pedagogy of the Oppressed*, written in 1968, the question of hope is considered a key issue in the process of emancipatory education. Paulo Freire strongly affirms the close bonds that unite despair and silence, therefore hope and speaking out:

Figure 1. Mural quoting Paulo Freire's Pedagogy of the Oppressed (artist unknown)

To glorify democracy and to silence the people is a farce; to discourse on humanism and to negate man is a lie. Nor yet can dialogue exist without hope. Hope is rooted in men's incompleteness, from which they move out in constant search - a search which can be carried out only in communion with other men. Hopelessness is a form of silence, of denying the world and fleeing from it. The dehumanization resulting from an unjust order is not a cause for despair but for hope, leading to the incessant pursuit of the humanity which is denied by injustice. Hope, however, does not consist in folding one's arms and waiting. As long as I fight, I am moved by hope; and if I fight with hope, then I can wait.[2]

---

1   Paulo Freire, *Pedagogia da Esperança*, São Paulo: Paz e Terra, 1992.
2   Paulo Freire, *Pedagogy of the Oppressed*, New York: Continuum, 1993 (1970), chap. 3.

The importance given to this principle shows that his reflection is not reducible to an emancipatory conception of pedagogy to which it is often reduced, especially in the French-speaking world where only two of his books have been translated.[3] This reflection encompasses a broader and deeper vision of social development, public space and democracy.[4] Arousing and maintaining hope among the oppressed consists in developing, in a critical and collective dialogue, a regulatory ideal of a social order based on justice and coexistence, making it possible to fight against inequalities of sex, race and class and for environmental justice. Without such a revolutionary horizon, the social struggle can have no direction or meaning.

The originality of Freire's thought lies in the fact that hope cannot be reduced to the supposedly "realistic" anticipations of official institutions, nor to a distant utopia, ceaselessly pushed back to a bright future: it is built in the very process of collective reformulation of the space of the possible and the thinkable. The communication policy of hope thus refers to the action by which, in critical dialogue, humans can change themselves and transform their social conditions in order to produce a more just society.[5] This action is central not only to survive under conditions of oppression but also to understand, in the full sense of the term, the condition of one's fellow human beings.

The feeling of hope is, therefore, a disposition of the mind and body which is not innate but acquired. Such a disposition that cannot be acquired in institutions inclined to reproduce inequalities and prejudices, where the conditions for authentic dialogue are weak or even non-existent: it must be acquired in measures specially designed to break with what Freire calls the 'culture of silence', that is, the fact that the oppressed do not dare to speak in public.

The Freirian conception of hope invite to question the social conditions of hope, through what appears to be one of its *sine qua non* conditions: the imperative to give voice to the 'voiceless'. How to 'communicate hope', in order to allow those who do not feel empowered to speak publicly[6] to co-define an emancipatory horizon in which they would feel fully included? Although he avoids criticism of pleading for a disconnected utopia, by returning to political work *here and now*, does Paulo Freire not take the risk of seeing the social relations of domination return to the very heart of the dialogic systems that he calls for?

For a sociologist, this question echoes a dilemma reflected in Antonio Gramsci's famous formula: how to reconcile 'pessimism of intelligence' and 'optimism of will'?[7] Thinking about the social conditions of hope confronts us with one of the paradoxes to which any revolutionary political enterprise is exposed, whether it is carried out by parties, unions, associations,

3   Irène Pereira, *Paulo Freire, pédagogue des opprimés*, Paris : éditions Libertalia, 2017.
4   Ana Cristina Suzina and Thomas Tufte, 'Freire's vision of development and social change: Past experiences, present challenges and perspectives for the future', *International Communication Gazette*, 82.5, 2020, pp. 411-424.
5   Silvio Waisbord, 'Why Paulo Freire is a threat for right-wing populism: Lessons for communication of hope', *The International Communication Gazette*, 82.5, 2020, pp. 440-455.
6   Daniel Gaxie, 'Cognitions, auto-habilitation et pouvoirs des "citoyens"', *Revue française de science politique* 57.6, 2007, pp. 737-757.
7   Antonio Gramsci, *Prison Notebooks*, New York, Chichester, West Sussex, 1992 (1975), notebook n° 9.

social movements or 'transformative intellectuals'. Raising the collective aspirations of the dominated, through voluntarist calls for collective action, to change the unjust rules of the social game, isn't it taking a risk, by 'misadjusting their subjective hopes to their objective chances' as Pierre Bourdieu puts it,[8] in other words of giving birth to 'a mad hope', a hope that has every chance of being disappointed? Can we change the dispositions incorporated in despair by symbolic work alone, without transforming, by properly political action, the objective structure of unequal distribution of social opportunities?

As anthropologist James C. Scott showed in *Weapons of the Weak*, what characterizes the attitude of subordinate groups in general is not speaking out in an overtly agonistic way, but what he calls 'calculated conformity'[9]: the apparent adjustment to the order of things as the dominant would like to see it appear. It is only behind the scenes, far from the eyes and ears of the powerful, that the dominated indulge in expressing the 'hidden transcript', a discourse of criticism of power that they generally take meticulous care to conceal.[10] Therefore, what to do with these incorporated provisions inclining them to remain silent, which the dominated bring with them, including in measures intended to give them a voice?

In 2018 a research team which I belong to, organized in Paris an international conference,[11] in the presence of James C. Scott among others, that lead in 2021 to the publication of a collective book entitled *Giving voice to the "voiceless"? Social and discursive construction of a public problem*.[12] In this collective and interdisciplinary work, which brings together 23 chapters written by 31 authors, we have attempted to reverse the usual problematic through which researchers approach the question of the *voiceless* and their speaking out.

The social sciences have indeed largely focused on analyzing the apparent silence of the *voiceless*. They show that the latter are misnamed, in the sense that their word, often held to be negligible or discredited, underestimated or (self) censored, has no less existence and, sometimes, power. Peasants, casual workers, informal workers, the colonized, exiles, soldiers, prostitutes, sick children, young people from working-class neighborhoods: if these groups occupy dominated positions in social relations of class, race, gender, nation or generation, they are generally constituted as collectives by the very people who send them this offer to speak out. The book thus places the focus on the political work of these *symbolic rehabilitation* organizations[13] and on their actors - activists, artists and cultural professionals, administrative and political staff, teacher-researchers, workers and patients from the medico-social sector,

8   Pierre Bourdieu, *Sociologie générale, volume 2. Cours au collège de France 1983-1986*, Paris: Seuil/ Raisons d'Agir, 2016, pp. 308-309.
9   James C. Scott, *Weapons of the weak. Everyday forms of peasant resistance*, New Haven & London: Yale University Press, 1985, pp. 241-303.
10   James C. Scott, *Domination and the arts of resistance: hidden transcripts*, New Haven & London: Yale University Press, 1990.
11   https://sansvoix.sciencesconf.org/.
12   Benjamin Ferron, Emilie Née and Claire Oger (eds.), *Donner la parole aux « sans-voix » ? Construction sociale et mise en discours d'un problème public*, Rennes, Presses Universitaires de Rennes, 2021.
13   Claude Grignon, Jean-Claude Passeron, *Le savant et le populaire. Misérabilisme et populisme en sociologie et en littérature*, Paris : Le Seuil, 1989.

journalists, and communicators. They not only help to give meaning to these operations but also to provoke, configure and frame the discourses that are held there.

While these measures are far from functioning as tools that magically extract the dominated from relations of domination, those actors who wish to *give voice to the voiceless* can generally be credited with the intentions they declare. They help to reconfigure the rules of the political game by raising the level of aspirations for social change of the agents who are enlisted.

But the book invites the reader to take a double step back. First, take a step back from a non-reflective use of the expression *voiceless*. This preconception assumes the existence of a group of people defined by a specific form of symbolic deprivation. But isn't attributing to these groups the common, and principal, property of being *voiceless* before any examination, every chance of functioning as an act of institution and a subpoena?

The interrogative form of the books' title invites a second step back with the statement *giving voice to the voiceless*, which may have worked as a slogan for alternative media, for example.[14] By this interrogative turn, it is not so much a question of recalling the obstacles to freedom of expression produced by the contemporary strengthening of authoritarian regimes and authoritarianism in democratic regimes, nor the existence of multiple obstacles to having a public voice, including in the usual functioning of institutions which claim to be democratic. It is above all a matter of emphasizing the falsely consensual nature of this promise of giving the word. The implicit partitions that it operates in the social world (between the voiceless and those who have it; between the voiceless and those who give them a voice, etc.) and the lack of clear definition of the problem that it poses invite us to equip the analysis with sharper weapons than those offered by functionalist models of communication, the questioning of which boils down to: who *gives* or *takes* this word and through what channel? Who listens to it and with what effects?

One of the scientific ambitions that has accompanied the coordination of this volume is thus to make an original contribution to social science research devoted to the construction of public problems. This contribution is twofold. It is, on the one hand, to underline the importance of the processes of formulating public problems which must be considered as elements of their construction dynamics. The book also questions the conditions for the success of a *second generation* social problem[15]: the unequal distribution of opportunities for the public expression of opinions. What, at any given time, makes the lack of public voice by dominated or oppressed groups a problematic situation?

This singular *problematic* is not a simple reformulation of the classic problem of freedom of expression: it explicitly and politically raises the question of the practical conditions for

---

14   Benjamin Ferron. 'Giving Voice to the Voiceless? The Ambivalent Institutionalization of Minorities'
      Alternative Media in Mexico and Israel', n Isabelle Rigoni and Eugénie Saïtta (eds.), *Mediating cultural
      diversity in a globalised public space*, New York: Palgrave, 2012, pp. 135-152.
15   Malcom Spector and John I. Kitsuse, *Constructing Social Problems*, Menlo Park, CA: Cummings, 1977.

suspending, limiting, or even temporarily reversing the monopoly of the legitimate public voice. We have called it *the problem of equality of expression*.

The main scientific contribution of the book can be summarized as follows. Researchers usually distinguish between the *pedagogical model of authorized speech,* and the *revolutionary model of subversive speech*.[16] The first tends to characterize institutional arrangements where citizens can express themselves with the permission of the institutions, but where they seem unlikely to change the rules of distribution of their social opportunities. The second corresponds to the most politically and openly engaged actions that seek to change the rules of the game by raising the expression of grievances, modifying the legislative framework, the modalities of conducting public action or the fundamental principles of the functioning of the political and economic system.

Reading the various contributions to the book that we have brought together, invites us to add a third model that we call the *therapeutic model of offered speech*. Acknowledging the relative inability of existing democratic mechanisms to counterbalance social inequalities in terms of public voice, this political model of second-degree communication postulates the need to create counterweight structures which make it possible to encourage or even force the diversification of points of view in the spaces of public debates. The case studied by Julien Talpin of Community Organizers in Los Angeles (USA), gives an excellent illustration of how networks of activist organizations can bring step by step young colored people from poor neighborhood to publicly speak their mind about class and racial oppression.

It is not for us here to judge the political superiority of this or that model of the dominated taking a public voice. We can only point out that, depending on the case, the underlying *communication policy of hope* will be different. In the pedagogical model of authorized speech, the master fixes, in accordance with the rules of the institution s/he represents, the limits of the space of the thinkable and the sayable. Hope is corseted but can boast a certain *realism* in the sense that the institution predefines the *real*.[17] In the revolutionary model of subversive speech, the normative horizon in the name of which one fights, and for which one speaks out presupposes a radical break with the institutional rules in force. Hope keeps the struggle alive, but it risks becoming Millenarian utopianism. In the therapeutic model of the offered speech, which is closest to the thought of Paulo Freire, hope is not predefined by the institution or maintained by a revolutionary political body, but is based on the anthropological belief that, in alternative institutions promoting autonomy, humans can exchange knowledge and views on an equal footing and collectively define a desirable future.

The work of Paulo Freire thus appeals us not only as researchers and intellectuals but also as citizen and professional practitioners put in the position of *giving voice to the voiceless*. How to maintain political hope in a dark period marked by a global pandemic, the authoritarian

---

16   Jacques Defrance, '"Donner" la parole. La construction d'une relation d'échanges', *Actes de la recherche en sciences sociales*, 73, 1988, pp. 52-66.
17   Peter Berger and Thomas Luckmann, *The Social Construction of Reality: A Treatise in the Sociology of Knowledge*, New York: Anchor Books, 1966.

turn of representative governments, a drastic reinforcement of social inequalities, a major economic crisis and a climate crisis threatening all aspects of life? To speak of hope in this context, undoubtedly requires a certain *optimism of the will*. Paulo Freire's thought undeniably constitutes a good starting point for rebuilding, through dialogue, an emancipatory common sense whose political horizon is action here and now in favor of social and environmental justice. Giving a voice to the *voiceless* seems, from this point of view, a not sufficient but necessary condition to give hope to the hopeless.

COMMUNICATION AND HOPE: PRODUCING AUDIOVISUAL FROM THE PERSPECTIVE OF INDIGENOUS PEOPLES

ERIBERTO MONTALVO GUALINGA

My name is Eriberto Gualinga Montalvo. I am from the Quechua people of Sarayaku, located in the state of Pastaza in Ecuador. I work as an audiovisual producer from the perspective of indigenous peoples, with a particular focus on the problems that involve my people, who have been fighting for more than 40 years to defend the territory and against extractive companies and projects.

In 2002, I made a film called *I am a defender of the forest*,[1] in which I show the military struggle over oil that my people had to experience that year. There are several testimonies in defense of nature, the vision of development of indigenous peoples, about how they see Mother Earth. Since then, I have always addressed these issues, problems against nature, against native peoples.

In my documentaries, I have never used testimonies of regret. On the contrary, they are testimonies that give strength, testimonies that help people to understand, to make visible why nature is important, why the vision of indigenous peoples is important, why it is important to take into account the thinking of indigenous peoples. That is why I think that my videos contribute a lot to reflection, to raising awareness of the importance of how indigenous peoples, for many years, have been living with nature without destroying it, and are sending a message to the world that nature is very important, and its ecosystem is threatened by extractive interests.

Recently, I have been addressing several topics. For example, in 2017, I made a film called *The canoe of life*,[2] in which my community proposed to take a 12 meter canoe to the COP-21 event in Paris. From the forest to Paris. This seemed like a very important topic, and, in the film, I follow them with my camera and end up producing a documentary that gives a very important message to the world. That's what it's about, giving a message from the bottom up, from our community. That's why I make documentaries. In order to continue to survive, so that the struggle of indigenous peoples is known. Because, if I hadn't taken a camera and made these documentaries, who would have made them? Who would have addressed these issues? Maybe outsiders, other producers.

So, it is also about having a memory, a living memory for the community, so that the whole history of the struggle is not lost and, if possible, culture, stories, songs, medicine, legends, all this wealth that exists in nature, that exists in communities, but that is not known by the people

---

1   Available, with subtitles in English, at https://www.youtube.com/playlist?list=PLHyktZ-Pvh2iyJAV8yQJiGJH1rj4K6SLD.
2   Available, in Spanish, at https://vimeo.com/273674796.

who live in the city. For this reason, it is very necessary that the indigenous peoples themselves begin to tell their stories, in order, perhaps, to contribute a small grain of information to society that, perhaps, does not know, or even realize who inhabits the forests. And, within the forests, we, many native peoples, are living together, with everything that surrounds us. That is why listening to the voices of indigenous peoples is very important.

And how are we going to listen to the voices of indigenous peoples? By the same means of communication, a camera, a camcorder, photography. It all reaches, impacts. And much more when it is well made and produced by indigenous peoples themselves.

So, our job is to raise the awareness of the people of the city and also make, have a memory, a living heart of information for the people. That is why I have been working all these years, always talking about the importance of nature, always talking about the vision of the indigenous peoples.

In this year of 2021, we will premiere a film called *Helena de Sarayaku, Helena Sarayakumanta* would be in Quechua. It is my first feature film, it lasts 70 minutes, and we will see the possibility of broadcasting in all possible spaces, so that it can be seen everywhere. It is a film about young people, about the voices of young people against climate change.

I am very proud that you have granted this space and that, right from the forest, I am here in my house, with thatched roof, behind it is the forest, there are the neighbors too. And, from here, with satellite internet technology, I can address you, students, academics, and everyone who is reading. Yes, we can save the forest. Yes, we can live with the forest without destroying it. And that's what my videos are about, raising awareness, contributing information, to defend the Amazon.

ON HUMILITY: READING FREIRE WITH UBUNTU

COLIN CHASI

Introduction

Snow[1] notes that to be a humble person is to recognize your limitations, is to take those limitations seriously and to thereby foster a realism in your attitudes, in your behaviors regarding the self and regarding others. Paulo Freire valued humility. This valuing of humility informs the way he approached education. It is reflected in his concern to enable people to be humanized.

In this article, I will humbly accept Freire's plea to not merely bank his ideas. Instead, I shall discuss the value of humility in the quest for education. I shall do this with insights from the African moral philosophy of ubuntu. Drawing on ubuntu in this way has yet to be attempted.

In the course of developing this ubuntu-led perspective on my Freire-inspired interest in humility and education, I aim to contemplate the idea of enabling people to become the most that they can be, the uniqueness of human altruism, the idea that education may humanize people, the limiting of humanity in postcolonial settings, and how humility in communication for social change may lead to (re)humanization. Given the originality of the ubuntu angle applied here, this chapter is a valuable reminder of the continuing relevance of studying Freire.

Enabling people to become the most they can be

For Freire, the application of a banking method to education approaches students as automatons; it does not invite them to critically engage reality. It rather works against learners turning towards 'their ontological vocation to be more fully human.'[2]

Seeking to enable all people to become more fully human is an idea I find very attractive, perhaps because it speaks to a perspective that is central to the African moral philosophy of ubuntu.

Whereas contemporary writing on ubuntu associates it with forgiveness and reconciliation, the earliest written records on ubuntu, beginning in 1846—and for the next 100 odd years—tie ubuntu to expositions of humanness.[3] Indeed, 'in written sources published prior to the 1960s, ubuntu always seems to be defined as a human quality.'[4]

---

1   Nancy E. Snow, 2021. Theories of humility: An overview, in Mark Alfano, Michael P. Lynch and Alessandra Tanesini (eds) *The Routledge handbook of philosophy of humility*, London: Routledge, 2021, pp. 9--25.
2   Paulo Freire, Pedagogy of the Oppressed. New York: Continuum, 2000, p.74.
3   Christian B. N. Gade, 'The historical development of the written discourses on ubuntu', *South African Journal of Philosophy* 30(3) (2011): 303-329.
4   Christian B. N. Gade, 'What is Ubuntu? Different Interpretations among South Africans of African

Under ubuntu, we say that a person becomes more human through the ways in which that person engages with the world. In the obverse, under ubuntu, it is said that the humanity of a person is diminished to the extent that that person harms others. (Here the notion of others includes all that exists beyond the self.) Ubuntu teaches that a person is more fully a person whensoever a person behaves in a way that enhances others in the world.[5]

From the perspective of ubuntu, it is commonly understood that people humanize the world by acting in ways that enable themselves and others to flourish. As Archbishop Desmond Mpilo Tutu[6] famously points out: 'Harmony, friendliness, community are great goods. Social harmony is for us the *summum bonum* – the greatest good.' A key contribution of ubuntu, and African moral thinking in general, to global thought about human rights is the valuing of human solidarity. The African Charter on Human and Peoples' Rights, which was adopted in 1981 and entered into force in 1986, is the sole international legal charter that recognizes solidarity rights. Unlike other international human rights charters, it is not only concerned with individual liberty, or with socio-economic equality. It also emphases group rights by speaking of fraternity or solidarity as duties and rights.[7]

In the above brief discussion on ubuntu, I am valorizing how Freire called for an approach to education that humanizes people. A question that this should raise is: What does all of this say for what it means to be a human being?

To be human

Michael Tomasello, an evolutionary anthropologist who conducts experiments comparing behaviors of human infants and primates at the Max Plank Institute in Germany, is quite insightful in this regard. He teaches that unlike other animals, human beings are altruistic. Human cultures are formed on the basis of this altruism, albeit that this altruism, 'cooperativeness and helpfulness are, as it were, laid on top of [an evolutionarily necessary] self-interested foundation.'[8]

Altruism enables the establishment of what Tomasello[9] describes as a 'we orientation', by which people create joint projects that are characterized by shared intentionality. In short, for Tomasello, altruism is the basis for the human cooperative culture which enables humans to outcompete other animals though they may be faster or stronger than humans. In contrast, the cultures of other animals are based predominantly on imitation and other exploitative practices.[10]

descent', *South African Journal of Philosophy* 31(3) (2012): 484-503.
5   Desmond Tutu, *No Future Without Forgiveness*, New York: Doubleday, 1999, p.29.
6   Idem
7   Benjamin Elias Winks, 'A covenant of compassion: African humanism and the rights of solidarity in the African Charter on Human and Peoples' Rights', *African Human Rights Law Journal* 11 (2011): 447-464.
8   Michael Tomasello, *Why we cooperate*, London: MIT Press, 2009, p.4-5.
9   Michael Tomasello, *Origins of human communication*, London: MIT Press, 2010, p.6.
10   Michael Tomasello, *Why we cooperate*, p.XV-XVI.

The altruism that Tomasello sees as fundamental to human cooperative practices may also be recognized in Curry, Mullins, and Whitehouse's[11] finding that in sixty societies across the world, morality-as-cooperation guides practices of helping kin, helping your group, reciprocating, being brave, deferring to superiors, dividing disputed resources, and respecting prior possession. Morality-as-cooperation 'leads us to expect that this type of cooperative behavior—forming friendships, *participating in collaborative endeavors*, favoring your own group, and adopting local conventions—will be regarded as morally good'.[12]

Insofar as participation speaks of a set of practices that involves both acknowledging what we and others are capable of and granting how we and others deserve to have a share in the commonwealth, the above notes on altruism suggest that, for humans, participation is of immense and unique value. From this perspective it may be profitable to read participation as political—as raising questions of who gets what from whom, where, when, why and how.[13] These questions are foundational to the establishment of human moral orders[14] as 'culture is essentially [a] society's composite answer to the varied problems of life'.[15]

Because human culture develops by predominantly altruistic means that involve cooperative communication practices, it is founded on educational practices. These educational practices in turn say a great deal about how people can navigate the world with capabilities and freedoms. Without being a determining factor, education nevertheless informs how people can, do or may participate in societal processes. This is one way to understand how education expresses, enables, and governs participation in ways that are political.

People are violently dehumanized wherever they are denied possibilities to participate in matters that concern them.[16]

Education and being less or more human

Denial of an education is an act of violence. To deny a people education and its epistemic benefits is an act of political violence that exposes such people to harms that could have been avoided. Such violence alienates people from cultures, that would be historically and contemporaneously developed to enable them to ratchet themselves up and beyond

11   Oliver Scott Curry, Daniel Austin Mullins and Harvey Whitehouse, 'Is It Good to Cooperate? Testing the Theory of Morality-as-Cooperation in 60 Societies', *Current Anthropology* 60(1) (2019): 47-69.
12   Idem, pp. 47-48; emphasis added.
13   Harold D. Lasswell, *Politics; Who Gets what, when, how*, New York: Whittlesey House McGraw-Hill Book Co, 1936.
14   Michael Tomasello, *A natural history of human morality,* Cambridge, M.A.: Harvard University Press, 2016.
15   Steve Biko, *I write what I like*. Johannesburg: Picador Africa, 2017, p. 107.
16   Lewis R. Gordon, 'Fanon's tragic revolutionary violence', in Lewis R. Gordon, T. Denean Sharpley-Whiting and Renée T. White (eds) *Fanon: A critical reader*, Cambridge, M.S.: Blackwell,1996, pp. 297-308.

hardships. On this view, evidently, education is fundamental to the recognition, preservation, and pursuit of human dignity. It is not just about the regurgitation of ABCs.

As a moral matter, education enables people to engage with the world in ways that enable them to live well with others in the world. As such education requires the individual to exercise critical consciousness that reads and writes the world in ways that affirm their choices, freedoms, agency, and dignity. Education places the individual at the center of their existence, affirming that they are undeniable participants in matters that concern them. For this reason, one may say that participation is about education. And education is about participation.

But individuals always find that their agency is bounded by circumstantial factors. To be human is to always be in relationship with others (that include all that counts as one's environment). In this respect people cannot exercise their choices and freedoms without fetter. People are bound to live lives that have the structure of bad faith in appearance,[17] where bad faith is 'the effort to hide from oneself, to hide from one's freedom and responsibility' as they seek to express themselves amid circumstances that both enable and impinge upon their modes of being.[18]

The course of an education should lead people to understand how such bad faith arises. Education should enable people to read their ways of being and not being amidst phenomena of the world. It should enable the individual, at the point of encountering others, to humbly reflect that 'there are neither utter ignoramuses nor perfect sages; there are only people who are attempting, together, to learn more than they now know'.[19]

The limiting of humanity in postcolonial contexts

For those who live in postcolonial worlds, it is important to say that colonial practices—including apartheid—are characteristically narcissistic. Colonized territories are made to imagine themselves and to adopt reflections of histories, epistemes and other forms of practices and modalities of being that are Western. In this sense, the post colony arises as a space in which a specific system of signs plays off against each other with a peculiar 'way of fabricating simulacra or re-forming stereotypes'.[20] When it comes to educational processes (including research processes), colonial *epistemicidal* praxes work such that all that is researched merely serves to 'other' the colonized.[21] In general, as was the case with the colony,[22] the post colony and its peoples get their deep meanings with reference to the

---

17   Jean-Paul Sartre, *Being and Nothingness: A phenomenological essay on ontology*, trans. H. E. Barnes, New York: Washington Square, 1956, p.89.
18   Lewis R. Gordon, *Fanon and the crisis of European Man: An essay on philosophy and the human sciences*, New York: Routledge, 1995, p.16-17.
19   Paulo Freire, Pedagogy of the Oppressed, p. 90.
20   Achiles Mbembe, *On the postcolony*, Berkeley, C.A.: University of California, 2001, p.102.
21   Idem, p.11.
22   Frans Fanon, *Black skin, white masks*, London: Pluto, 1986.

Western.[23] All this might in some part explain the acuity of the falsity that marks its cultural life[24] insofar as cultural life is founded on denial of the existence of colonized people.

Søren Kierkegaard[25] metaphorically lamented that influenced by the media of his time, people were splashing about in shallow waters pretending that they were in great peril. Now too, contemporary colonized researchers and educators splash around in shallow waters of the satisfactions of others, pretending they are overcoming great perils. Yet research they produce normally fails to address everyday needs such as those occasioned by the HIV/AIDS pandemic.

It is vital to advocate for decolonial education as a process that allows people with critical consciousness to humbly reject further manipulation and violation;[26] refuse oppression and its humiliation; and instead find dignity and worth in new cooperative practices that meet their needs.[27] Such education empowers the oppressed to advance dialogue that 'requires an intense faith in humankind, faith in their power to make and remake, to create and re-create, faith in their vocation to be more fully human (which is not the privilege of an elite, but the birthright of all)'.[28] Such education affirms and draws on the realization of the power of human culture to ratchet people out of misery, subjugation and other avoidable forms of hardships and misfortune. It embraces and makes use of the ways in which human beings are socially birthed into altruistic possibilities.

This following and concluding section will briefly outline Freire-influenced ideas on how communication for social change may, with humility, catalyze the (re)humanization of societies that are laden with colonialism, apartheid, and their legacies.

Towards humility and humanization in communication for social change

Communication for social change has been indelibly influenced by Freire. After working in the field for over twenty years, I can say that in South Africa, from where I am writing, Freire is the foundational figure around whom scholarship for communication for social change is built.

A challenge for many who are placed in positions of leading communication for social change efforts in South Africa, as in other postcolonial settings, is that the processes

---

23   cf. Mbembe, 2001.
24   Mbembe, 2001, p.375.
25   Soren A. Kierkegaard, 'The Present Age', trans. A. Dru, in R. Brettal (ed) *A Kierkegaard Anthology*, Princeton, N.J.: Princeton University, 1947 (1846), pp. 258-269.
26   Carl Stauffer, 'Humility, forgiveness, and restorative justice: From the personal to the political', in Mark Alfano, Michael P. Lynch and Alessandra Tanesini (eds) *The Routledge handbook of philosophy of humility*, London: Routledge, 2021, p.165.
27   Paulo Freire, 'The adult literacy process as cultural action for freedom', *Harvard Educational Review* 68 (1998): 1-44.
28   Paulo Freire, Pedagogy of the Oppressed, p.90.

that legitimate them to assume leadership roles are greatly guided by Western logics. Leadership is often granted based on achievements in Western systems of education, or by reason of the leader having excelled in manipulating some aspects of the colonial dominant systems. In all instances, an upshot is that practitioners may be resented by the colonized as they inadvertently or otherwise symbolize the loss of native sovereignty, and thus represent the victory of the colonial enterprise and its claims regarding the superiority of Western rationality.[29] Indeed, in their struggles to end colonial domination, 'the imperial lord and the colonial bondsman leave marks on each other....'.[30]

Inevitable ways in which the colonized are tied up with their colonizers lead, for example, to Black medical practitioners being treated by fellow colonized peoples with both pride and hatred.[31] Recognizing this, Colin Chasi,[32] who is greatly influenced by Freire, has argued that it is important for practitioners of communication for social change to grant that those who are subjected to such communication are knowledgeable agents whose choice, freedom, and agency matter. From this perspective, Chasi calls for a co-creative approach to rethinking, renaming, and rebuilding societies in ways that advance social justice. This turn to co-creation is not possible if the practitioner of communication for social change assumes a narcissistic stance. But this turn to co-creation is possible if the practitioner humbly recognizes that the road to a better world is made by the footsteps of all who walk it.[33]

An approach that says that practitioners of communication for social change should embrace the targets of their communication as co-creators of the new and desired realities does not assert an idea of humility that eviscerates practitioners' expertise and possibilities to contribute positively to social processes. In this regard, there is value to briefly saying something about Samantha Vice's interesting paper titled *How Do I Live in this Strange Place*. Vice, a white South African, suggests that given the history of apartheid it is necessary for white South Africans to humble themselves. She suggests they do this by assuming a posture of silence to allow others to speak. She progressively accepts that the oppressed of her postcolonial world can and do speak. Further, she posits that the oppressed are not heard because their voices are drowned out the narcissism which makes colonial voices so loud, which would be valid in some ways. But I take issue with her suggestion that the solution to creating a more just South Africa is to silence white compatriots. Instead, drawing from Paulo Freire, I suggest that all people (black, white and beyond these binary identity-logics) need to learn humility, the humility to not just place ourselves as teachers, but to also place ourselves in positions where we accept that we are also learners. All teachers are learners, and all learners are teachers. With such

---

29   Frans Fanon, *A dying colonialism,* trans. H. Chevalier, Harmondsworth, Middlesex: Penguin, 1970, p.111-2.
30   Ngugi wa Thiong'o, *Globaletics: Theory and the politics of knowing*, New York: Columbia University Press, 2012, p.51.
31   Frans Fanon, *A dying colonialism*, p.113.
32   Colin Chasi, *Hard Words: On communication on HIV/AIDS*, Johannesburg: Real African Publishers, 2011.
33   Myles Horton and Paulo Freire, *We make the road by walking: Conversations on education and social change*, ed. B. Bell, J. Gaventa and J. Peters, Philadelphia: Temple University, 1990.

humility it is possible to reclaim the altruistic source of human cultural, cooperative agency to build a more just world. From this Freirean position, it is possible for those who come from privileged-legitimated backgrounds to have the humility to allow those who come from disadvantaging-delegitimated backgrounds to make their contributions so that an educational and socially productive engagement takes place.

Postcolonial worlds are paradigmatically strange places. They are places in which the estrangement of one from another is normalized. Narcissistic colonialism prevents the participation of others in the elaboration of societies that flourish. It limits the normalization of loving, respecting, granting dignity. In contrast, if they are to co-elaborate a more humanized world into being, communication for social change practitioners must 'dare to say scientifically… that we study, we learn, we teach, we know with our entire body. We do all of these things with feeling, with emotion, with wishes, with fear, with doubts, with passion, and also with critical reasoning… never with the last only'.[34] Doing this while also enabling others to fully engage with the world of their concerns requires humility.[35]

A question that remains is, should the oppressed too be humble? Is it decent to ask the oppressed to be humble? Freire[36] offers the view that the humble ideal is for the dominated to save their dominators by saving themselves. He elaborates that, in the process of emancipating themselves, the oppressed shall set everybody free, that the oppressed are the only ones who can do this. This is a remarkable thing to think and say. It is also something that can be well understood by thinking rather idealistically about the immense power and authority that comes with the humility of the oppressed who do not have time to trifle with pride, to mistreat others for no good reasons, or to not be deeply committed to the creation of a better tomorrow for themselves and for everybody else. Such oppressed people can realize that humility with altruism will set everybody free. This Freirean perspective on the humble role of the oppressed in setting everyone free is itself an affirmation of the dominant contemporary view that says, with ubuntu, that the oppressed can forgive and reconcile with their oppressors to build more just worlds.[37] This affirms that the humble oppressed have much to teach the world—and communication for social change has a powerful educational role in enabling this.

---

34   Paulo Freire, 'The adult literacy process as cultural action for freedom', p.3.
35   Robert Roberts, 'Humility and human flourishing', in Mark Alfano, Michael P. Lynch and Alessandra Tanesini (eds) The Routledge handbook of philosophy of humility, London: Routledge, 2021, p.54; 57.
36   Paulo Freire, 'The adult literacy process as cultural action for freedom', p.13.
37   see Desmond Tutu, No Future Without Forgiveness.

FREIREAN 'HUMILITY' IN THE AGE OF THE PROLIFERATING SPECTACLE: A REFLECTION

ANITA GURUMURTHY

I was introduced to Paulo Freire as a student in the late 80s. The Department of Education in India had introduced a pathbreaking feminist program shaped by feminists and femocrats. Inspired by the Freirian idea of 'conscientization'[1] and the Gramscian notion of 'subalternity',[2] this was a radical adult literacy endeavor to remedy the historical neglect of women in mass education; especially those women who bear the brunt of caste and religious discrimination in the Indian society. The Mahila Samakhya Programme,[3] as it was called, envisioned the *sangha* – or the women's collective – as the central infrastructure, the Freirian 'cultural circle'[4] for critical pedagogy. The *sangha* was women's own space for critical thinking, reflection, and plotting collective action. It was a perfect case of indigenization of an idea with universal applicability. The program had far reaching [impacts on the educational enrollment of girls,[5] with tens of thousands of *sangha* women daring to dream of a better future for their daughters.

Much later in time, my organization, IT for Change, began a small-scale experiment with *sangha* women in Mysuru district – a project that we continue to work on. It is hard not to be moved by Frierian thought. Its piercing love and enduring meaning provide new ways to open up and scrutinize today's contradictions and tomorrow's destiny. So, in keeping with the spirit of the Mahila Samakhya Programme, we brought in digital technologies into the *sangha* ecosystem. Our intent was to facilitate critical pedagogies for the *sangha*. In Freirian terms, we were offering a new language of critique. With a new repertoire of information, knowledge, and communication strategies – Dalit women stormed the Brahminized local public sphere with their own dialects on public radio broadcasts through the *Kelu Sakhi*[6] program; boldly curated, archived, and disseminated their stories on video clips;[7] set up information centers[8] that have become vanguard local institutions; thus, building *sangha*-managed systems to renegotiate

---

1   Concepts Used by Paulo Freire, Freire Institute, https://www.freire.org/paulo-freire/concepts-used-by-paulo-freire.
2   Antonio Gramsci, 'Critical Explorations in Contemporary Political Thought', in Guido Liguori, *Conceptions of Subalternity in Gramsci*, London: Palgrave Macmillan, 2015, pp. 118-133, available at: https://link.springer.com/chapter/10.1057%2F9781137334183_7.
3   Mahila Samakhya Programme, Ministry of Human Resource and Development, https://www.education.gov.in/en/mahila-samakhya-programme.
4   Jeongbong Cho, 'The Educational Practice of the 'Cultural Circle' Organized by Paulo Freire', *Philosophy of Education* (2017), http://journal.kci.go.kr/pesk/archive/articleView?artiId=ART002240044.
5   Madhumita Bandyopadhyay and Ramya Subrahmanian, 'Gender Equity in Education: A Review of Trends and Factors', *Create Pathways to Access Research Monograph No 18*, 2008, http://www.create-rpc.org/pdf_documents/PTA18.pdf.
6   *Sanghada Sangati Kelusakhi* (dir. Aparna Kalley and Chinmayi Arakali, 2007), available at: https://youtu.be/OqNIk0XnaPw.
7   *Namma Akkandira Nodi* (dir. Savitha Kumari T S, 2008), available at: https://youtu.be/TyqWmiXv5Io.
8   *Beyond ICT Access - Creating Empowering Cultures of Use with Dalit Women* (2015), available at: https://youtu.be/_zDzUCZCQxM.

political power.

The work is in perpetual flux — a symbol both of the vibrant resilience of the oppressed and the obdurate tenacity of oppressive historical structures. Our work has since grown with a clear, inter-generationalfootprint[9] in Mysuru, as granddaughters of *sangha* women have become feminist digital curators.

There are no easy metrics to evaluate the success of our interventions. Patriarchy has not disappeared, and caste is still a loud and clear reality. Communal fault lines run deep in the social fabric. The *sangha* itself is a tenuous collective caught in the forceful winds of state policies under neoliberalism that leave overworked women in extreme precarity with little time or resources to enjoy the conviviality of association, the luxury of collective deliberation, and a politics of sustained action. But as women often tell us, *they are finding liberation on their own terms,* even if it means allowing men their illusions.[10]

The leaders who have facilitated the community processes — members of the oppressed classes themselves — are Freire's ideal type of the 'becoming human'.[11] They, as Freire would say, are 'making *the road by walking'*.[12]

Our experiments with conscientization also extend to urban youth in situations of poverty and marginality — building their capabilities for critical thinking about techno-social architectures, creativity, and leadership. Through Spoorthi,[13] we set up a community-managed data system for grievance redressal; through Nan Voice Nan Choice,[14] a local language community radio show, we are working to support identity-building among school girls in early adolescence; with the Youth Resource Centre of Samvada, we worked on a local language campaign[15] against online misogyny; with teachers in local schools across different Indian states, we have unleashed the power of **contextual resource,**[16] *and at a meta level, our work has sought to bring to social movements the* **digital analysis**[17] *needed for them to navigate their struggles.*

---

9   *Dhwanigalu: Stories of Change* (dir. Shreeja K., 2017), available at: https://youtu.be/uftj4xZHudE.
10   Kameshwari Jandhyala, 'Empowering Education: the Mahila Samakhya Experience', *Feminist Law Archives*, https://feministlawarchives.pldindia.org/wp-content/uploads/Empowering-Education.pdf.
11   John Holst, 'Paulo Freire as Learning Theorist', Adult Education Research Conference, Buffalo, New York, https://newprairiepress.org/cgi/viewcontent.cgi?article=4153&context=aerc.
12   Myles Horton and Paulo Freire, *We Make the Road by Walking: Conversations on Education and Social Change*, Philadelphia, Pennsylvania: Temple University Press, 1990.
13   IT for Change, 'Introducing 'Spoorthi': A Spatial Data System for the Inclusive Cities Agenda in India', *Medium*, 16 January 2019, https://medium.com/field-stories/introducing-spoorti-a-spatial-data-system-for-the-inclusive-cities-agenda-in-india-c02d1da8c9a0.
14   Nan Voice, Nan Choice: Community Radio Program, Hosa Hejje, Hosa Dishe, https://itforchange.net/hosa-hejje-hosa-dishe/.
15   IT for Change, Participatory Action Research on Gender-Based Hate Speech Online with a Karnataka-Based Youth Group', *IT for Change*, 2021, https://itforchange.net/sites/default/files/1738/PAR-on-gender-based-hate-speech-online-with-a-Karnataka-based-youth-group.pdf.
16   Professional Learning Communities through the Subject Teacher Forum, IT for Change, https://itforchange.net/index.php/professional-learning-communities-through-subject-teacher-forum.
17   A Digital New Deal: Visions of Justice in a Post-Covid World, https://itforchange.net/digital-new-deal/.

As the elite outsiders in the process, our role has been to create an interstice – a liminal space – between lived reality on the one hand and curiosity, reflection, faith, and hope on the other, through multiple critical literacies that include grappling with the dominant structures even as we engage with the alternative. This, in Freirian terms, may be seen as the space of 'epistemological knowing'[18] – a space that we strive to deepen also for ourselves in fashioning our praxis and engaging with local-to-global processes of institutional and policy change.

A learning organization

As a learning organization, we see life under digital capitalism along three axes – the alienated self, mob truth, and techno-structures of oppression – that urge a rethinking for a just social order. These intersecting axes are elaborated below.

Digitality – locked within the imperialist economic paradigm – produces through its platform publics a narcissistic self. Networked individualism is based on a fragile subjectivity in perpetual search of belonging. A sociality subsumed within capitalist platforms means, like Freire's peasants, we are all alienated from our own authentic agency. The faith and hope to attain our humane potential are entrapped in a 'banking method'[19] of public engagement – a colonizing culture of datafied interactions that anchor our choice and destiny in the circuits of digital capitalism.

The network is ruthless; its anti-dialogic ephemerality dehumanizes social interaction. And the datafied individual is but an ever-multiplying object in an expanding commodity market of diversity. This is the self in a post social digitality – excavated of reflection, empathy, humility.

There is then the mob that thrives on the algorithmic sorting apparatus scaffolding the online publics. Assuming an invulnerability antithetical to a dialogic public, the mob delegitimizes experiences of oppression, creating vehement fictions, erasing any vestige of voice from the margins. The mob polarizes the space of the public arrogantly and relentlessly. It engenders a culture of violence that silences the 'outgroup' – that is, those who seek to assemble a memory that is different from the mob's hegemonic truth. Feeding violence into the network, and riding on the network's mind-numbing virality, the mob flattens public discourse into virulent, singular narratives – each of which systematically disarticulates the outgroup's claims. In our research at IT for Change,[20] we found a worrisome impact of the normalized sexism that young women in India face in the online publics; most of them recalibrated their public political personas, moving towards a gender conservative presence to gain social acceptance in digital society.

The network is an antithesis of the safe Freirian space of epistemological distance – 'where there are no themes or values of which one cannot speak, no areas in which one must be

18   Paulo Freire, *Pedagogy of the Oppressed*, trans. Myra Bergman Ramos, London: Penguin Classics, 2017.
19   Paulo Freire, *Pedagogy of the Oppressed*.
20   Anita Gurumurthy, Amrita Vasudevan, Nandini Chami, 'Born Digital, Born Free? A Socio-Legal study on Young Women's Experiences of Online Violence in South India', *IT for Change*, 2019, https://itforchange.net/sites/default/files/1618/Born-Digital_Born-Free_SynthesisReport.pdf.

silent'.[21] The testimonies and memories of those who seek to reclaim their place in the world do not count. Memory is but a patchwork of quantified presence and fabricated truths. And knowing, no longer a social process of the multiple Freirian thinking subjects. There is no room in the mob's truth for any humility.

This brings us to the structures of oppression in digitality – our shared condition as subjects entangled in a society of the spectacle that is permanently mutating, integrating, and disintegrating –ever-multiplying.

Like the mathematical system of virality that sustains it, oppression in the times of digital media is fractal. Its spatio-temporal dimensions invade the deeply private spaces, even the soul, of the oppressed. Just think of how algorithms discipline taxi drivers, extracting their labor, and laboring data – taking control of their life space.

Freire writes about how the oppressed find in the oppressor their model of 'manhood'[22] or their model of humanity, of what it means to be a free person. The aura of planetary life under Artificial Intelligence (AI) dichotomizes the world – dividing the intelligent economies from those that must play catch up. Like the peasants who thought that to be free meant aspiring to be like their oppressive landowners, nations that wish to embrace the digital seem to claim their digital futures in the image of the hegemonic model that unabashedly dares to play with human futures – encoding, engulfing, and enslaving planet and people for profit.

The power to control the soul of society is a heady one. Jeff Bezos never wanted to sell books, he always wanted to sell everything. Arrogant entrepreneurialism over valorized as innovation – so capitalism can move fast and break things – has ossified non-humility as the base structure of the network. Faith and hope are no longer human. Trust is a blockchain-based techno-artefact, and wisdom, the creative improbabilities of machine learning models.

The structures of digital capitalism do not just delegitimize alternate narratives. They normalize a social violence that cripples the very ability to imagine different digital futures. They condemn democracy to a delusional grandeur in which trust has no place, humility no value. There is only authority and control.

But in our faith and humility, we have to claim hope.

As Freire believed, the naming of the world, through which people constantly re-create that world, cannot be an act of arrogance. The social movements of the decade coinciding with the digital age – from the student movements in South Africa, India, and Chile; the #MeToo movement led by ordinary women around the world; and the clear voices of Black Lives Matter and the Muslim women of Shaheen Bagh – all show, a deep failure of current institutions.

---

21   Paulo Freire, Teachers as Cultural Workers - Letters to Those Who Dare Teach, trans. Donoldo Macedo, Dale Koike, and Alexandre Oliveira, Boulder, CO: Westview Press, 1998, p. 58.
22   Freire, Pedagogy of the Oppressed.

As Freire would say, history is made by definitive choices. The choices that can unlock the idea of societies that provide the opportunity for the highest possible humanness – for everybody. Unless the violence of the current system is recognized, unless the institutions of democracy can reshape the culture of public reasoning, adopting a pluralistic sensibility inherent in Freirian thinking,[23] unless institutions can reinvent themselves through humility and dialogue, democracy will be lost to digital fundamentalism.

Freire's Pedagogy of the Heart,[24] also reminds us that to be humble is to acknowledge that emotions are central to the process of conscientization. This goes right into the core of our institutional systems – our governments, universities, schools, scientific establishments – and how they can program for a new digitality grounded in the non-dualism that Freire advocated; how institutional cultures can ignite the emergence of a liberated society that does not dichotomize thinking and feeling, human and non-human, physical and virtual.

On the part of social movements this needs a vision of how citizenship can be obtained through a never-finished openness that Freirian philosophy demands for the good fight. For organizations in the space of changemaking, such humility is, as Freire argues, 'a matter of studying reality that is alive, reality that we are living inside of, reality as history being made and also making us'.[25] It is about contemplating the digital mediation of life – and what might it mean *to become human* in a digitally connected reality that is, itself, *alive*[26] and what it will take as a society to bring that privilege to all.

---

23   Kim Díaz, *Radical Democracy in the Thought and Work of Paulo Freire and Luis Villoro*, PhD Diss., Texas
      A&M University, Texas, 2012, available at: http://oaktrust.library.tamu.edu/bitstream/handle/1969.1/
      ETD-TAMU-2012-05-11133/DIAZ-DISSERTATION.pdf.
24   Paulo Freire, *Pedagogy of the Heart*, trans. Donaldo P. Macedo, Alexandre Oliveira, Continuum, 1997.
25   Paulo Freire, 'Reading the World and Reading the Word: An Interview with Paulo Freire', *Language Arts*,
      62(1), 1985, pp. 15-21, available at: https://www.jstor.org/stable/41405241.
26   Dario Torre, Victoria Groce, Richard Gunderman, et al., 'Freire's View of a Progressive and Humanistic
      Education: Implications for Medical Education', *MedEdPublish*, 6(3), available at https://doi.
      org/10.15694/mep.2017.000119.

EATING, DRINKING, DANCING, SINGING AND LIFTING THE SKY

AILTON KRENAK

This voracious violence that surrounds us, is deeply affecting *being*, which is not collective. It is *being* in the singular sense, in the most existential sense. It is each person, each individual. So, the radicality of this subject needs an answer in a chaotic world. It is as if each of us has become a particle and that particle is full of needs, expectations, desires. And there is a madness. But the world also became a particle. Our own idea of a world that coordinates bodies, elements, and subjects, is diluted in this time of violence, in several ways.

That expression that is invoked to express structural racism, that kind of intersection, the super layers of an event that affects the same body, it is a truth of the time that we are living in now, in which the same subject is subjected to questions that are domestic - the relationship with the family, with children, with mothers, with grandparents, with this nucleus that produces affections, that generates meaning, that institutes meaning – for people that are dispersed on several continents. And as we are dispersed on several continents, we still suffer another cleavage, which is cultural.

We are spread over several continents and immersed in different cultures. These different cultures establish different meanings for life. So, when we think that life, that wonderful and inexplicable sensation that we experience, is something total, that my life is like the life of that rock there, like the life of that bird, like the life of that guy who is walking there in Africa or in China, we are also at risk of generalization.

Because this experience of living, for each of us, is so different, is so incommunicable that, when we ignore cultural boundaries, when we sublimate the worldview differences that each people, that each set of people, that each idea of community that we elaborate, can express, we are again building an ideal world.

We build ideal worlds when we sublimate diversity, complexities, difference. We are radically different from each other, despite the fact that we move constantly, from the point of view of education, from the point of view of forming mentalities, towards wanting to be equal. There is a call, which may come from the time when the idea of modernity was installed, that we are going to move towards a commonality, a state of equality. And nothing in nature tells us about this move towards a state of equality.

Everything in nature explodes in diversity. So, we humans - if we can build a shared human idea - we humans are radically diverse because we are of nature. We are not separated from nature. We insist on separating ourselves from nature, when we seek this idea of unity, that we are all equal.

The idea of equality, fraternity, these civilizing foundations, they act in a movement contrary to everything that nature does. It is as if we humans insist on having a different signal from nature. If we continue with this different signal from nature, insisting on the production of equality between us, without being aware that this equality needs to be sown in the field of diversity, in the recognition of difference, in the possibility of a radical difference, we will always find a turning on the path, which will return us to the same place.

I was, once, walking in the forest, in a region that I didn't know, in the Amazon. We had gone to the territory of an indigenous people to visit my relatives there, and I had two non-indigenous friends with me, two people from the city with me. When we finished the visit to that village, we set out on our way back and there was a long stretch where we had to pass through the forest. The other option was to take a canoe and go down the river by canoe for a longer period. But we wanted to take the shortest route. My friends insisted that I go with them, on foot, cutting my way through the forest. And they were very confident that I would be able to guide them through that crossing into the forest. And they insisted and I ended up giving in. I said 'ok', and they played with me saying 'of course, with you, we're going through this forest'.

And we left. The day was already ending and my relatives in that village said, 'be careful not to let it get dark with you inside the forest, because you don't know the forest and there is a jaguar there'. So, my friends said, 'we are going quickly, we are going to arrive before nightfall'. I, much more involved with being friends with them, accepted this risk, and we entered the trail, we took a path. On the way, after we had walked for several hours, they were euphoric when they saw a clearing, because there was a house there, a small house. And they were euphoric, saying 'we are arriving'. In fact, we hadn't walked a third of the way and we stopped at this yard. The elder who lived there, he knew me, greeted us with great joy, invited us to eat or drink something and said to us, 'you are going to stay here, at home, today, right?'. And we said 'no, we're leaving'. He said 'look, if I were you, I would stay here and tomorrow I would continue traveling, because you are far away'. When I looked, my two colleagues had already gone out of the yard and were already entering the forest, saying to me 'let's go'. And I went with them.

The night before, it had rained, rain in the forest, and the rain had knocked over a big tree. And the tree had blocked the trail on which the Indians walked. Now, we had a crown of a big tree, fallen on the only trail that we could follow. One of my friends, very daring, decided to go around the tree and picked the trail, going around the tree. In a little while, he shouted euphoric 'wow, I found a way'. And we, satisfied with the path he had found, comfortable with the path he had found, were amazed, saying 'wow, we were walking on such a dense trail'. Suddenly, our friend found a veritable avenue within the forest. And we were walking along that path that, clearly, had been cleared, and that someone had used a sickle, a machete, and cleared the path, which is used by rubber tappers to cut rubber, inside the forest.

But the rubber cutting path makes an eight, it draws a figure eight. And we were exactly getting into an eighth leg. And we walked, in the eight, for four hours, back and forth. Until one of our colleagues said, 'I've seen this tree, I've seen this tree'. Then, one, more irritated, said 'of course you saw this tree, we are inside the forest, it is full of trees here', irritated. I observed and said that 'he is saying that he has seen this tree, because this tree is scratched, it is scratched because someone cut this tree to get latex from the rubber tree, this is a marked rubber tree'. And the other said 'no, let's keep going'. And we walk. We probably did five laps of the figure eight.

With that, came nightfall. And now, we were inside the forest, lost in an eight, which would be, more or less, the parable of us moving through this world, full of complexity, which could be thought of as a forest, but that, from time to time, we imagine that we have found a vast, wide trail for us to follow, even playing along the way, singing along the way. But we are not seeing that we are making a figure eight.

I have an impression that, from the end of the 20th century until the turn of the 21st century, we were strongly urged to adopt this idea of finding a way, to find a way that could put us all in that common place. This globalization event, it is a terrible reality, because, while it is an event, it is also an advertisement. It is an event because it preceded our perception that there was a globalizing event. And globalization, it happened above our heads, I mean, it happened beyond our observation. It is a phenomenon that integrates the global financial system, that integrates the decision management system of global governance. It is totalitarian and we salute it as if it were progress. Something is coming over there, ahead of us. Look, it looks like we've arrived.

In fact, we've been on an eight since the turn of the 20th century and some observers think that the 20th century isn't over yet, that we're still turning around in the 20th century, with the same mentality and the same perspectives of an industrial humanity, industrial, technological, and moving further and further away from the Earth.

The Earth, she calls, calls, calls people to be diverse, to be immersed in a diversity so potent that it produces, of itself, other diversities. It multiplies in diversity. And we insist, mentally, on unity. We insist. The way of governing the world wants to be unity. The way of managing our conflicts wants to be unity. So, it is a trend that opposes unity to diversity.

This tendency, which is common to many peoples, to oppose unity to diversity, has confused us a lot. Many people who tried to help us, thinking, Paulo Freire, for example, he lived in a period of history, of this history that we are considering as a kind of portal of globalization, but, personally, he did not live the experience of globalization. Globalization, it was an event that coincided with the passing of this man, this great thinker, and I wonder what Paulo Freire would say about globalization, globalization not as a future possibility, but as an event today, with a pandemic killing millions of people around the world, replacing his analysis, which were political conflicts, which were ideological conflicts, which were conflicts between peoples. How would Paulo Freire think of a conflict between humanity and the planet, the Anthropocene?

I think he was quite right, when he was able to deal with intra-human conflicts, because these intra-human conflicts, they are defined by our culture, by our ideologies, by our ideas, so to speak of religion, by worldviews that can be reconciled. Because a worldview is not exclusive. Worldviews are capable of dialogue.

Despite this insistence on separating East and West, the very idea of inventing a West and inventing an East, is much more a necessity of our mind to create departments, boxes, than a reality. Observing the climate, nature, and the landscape, is an open book that the Earth offers us, since humans walk around here. We and all other beings are, all the time, illustrated by a great book, which is the Earth, that wonderful organism. We, as much as we prepare for life, we continue to neglect the lessons that the Earth gives us. When some of our best thinkers of the twentieth century came up with ideas, proposals for cooperation between humans, they always did it with their faces turned towards the book that the Earth offers us to read.

The book of the Earth can be read with the body. Once visiting my friend Davi Kopenawa Yanomami, there in his territory, at a time when they were also having a hard time, because they were invaded by prospectors - as they are now, again -, I asked him 'cousin, what do you do to overcome these difficult periods of crisis that can make a person sick? '. He said, 'when I'm feeling great difficulty, I go into the woods, look for a clearing and lie on the ground, and I'm lying on the ground; and I wait for the forest to talk to me, the Earth to talk to me, I wait *Omam [the creator]* to talk to me; when *Omam* talks to me, it gives me everything I need to stay alive'. So, he connects his body with the body of the Earth, to read the Earth. How many of us are willing to read the Earth?

I remember that, when the possibility for a blind man to read was created, the Braille code; when Braille made it possible for a person without vision to read, it was so wonderful, because he could touch his finger and, in those marks, he could read, he could see the world. Now, perhaps, we need to stop being blind and put the body on the ground and read the Earth. Read the Earth and see if we can at least start with what the Earth says and reduce our madness for unity a little, which we think is possible, when what life and daily life has shown us is that nothing in the cosmos is repeated as equal. First of all, it is produced as a difference. And how wonderful difference. A difference that produces life. A life-producing power.

Some contemporary scientists of ours are already admitting that this cosmos and this Earth are alive, they are life, they are a code of life. If we manage to plug into this code of life, we can take a step in evolution. It is very interesting in Paulo Freire's centenary if someone alternates the word evolution with another one that he liked a lot, which was revolution. We need to evolve, not in the Darwinian sense, that many people took advantage of Darwin's theory to impose more conflict, more tension, and more inequality between us. An evolution that takes us to the meaning of life.

Life is metamorphosis. Life is evolution in that sense. A caterpillar, which is that bundle of stomachs, that bundle of digestive tracts, it does not know that it is going to be a butterfly. As Emanuele Coccia, that beloved contemporary philosopher and thinker, said, a caterpillar does not know that it will be a butterfly. That's what evolving is. We believe that we can become butterflies from caterpillars. What is also wonderful is that a butterfly does not remember that it was a caterpillar. So, long live the butterfly! And long live the caterpillar! Long live the difference that imprints on these bodies, with such distinction, that one flies and the other is an eating, eating, eating machine. Digestion, I don't know.

So, looking at the world with this tendency to difference, maybe it is moving towards producing affection, before wanting to produce equality. To produce affections is to recognize that the other can be as different from me as a caterpillar is different from a butterfly, but that neither denies that it has a shared origin in life, on Earth.

It is very interesting that a good part of the material that constitutes Paulo Freire's work is the relationship between human beings and the Earth. But what is interesting is that he was interested, or what he was watching was human labor. He was interested in the work that human beings do on Earth. It would be very interesting if we were able to observe the affection that human bodies can awaken on Earth. Instead of looking at Earth as a place of resources, look at Earth as a place of affection. Instead of human beings taking bread with sweat from the Earth, they are taking affection from the Earth with love.

This idea of humanity taking bread with sweat from the Earth is a very sad idea. It is sad that humanity has to take the bread out of the Earth with sweat. There is a romantic poetics on this theme, but for me, who am an Indian, who comes from a people who call the Earth 'my mother', we don't take anything from it with sweat. We suck it. The children of the Earth have her as their mother. They don't have to sweat anything out of it.

This idea of a civilization that needs to sweat to earn something from the Earth is an idea very close to the idea of a slave. We are not slaves to the Earth. We are children of the Earth. And children usually get food for free. This is affection.

Affection is not just a word. Affection is an experience. Eating, drinking, dancing, singing, and lifting the sky is a pedagogy, so to speak, of the Earth with its children. Eat, drink, dance, sing and lift the sky; eating, drinking, dancing, singing, and lifting the sky is an exercise in staying alive as a celebration of life. Life is to be celebrated. Life is not to be measured; life is not to be negotiated. Life has no *value*.

The idea that life is worth anything is a capitalist idea; it is an idea that wants to measure how old I am to see if I can already die or if I get a covid vaccine.

We are experiencing a trivialization of life on the planet when everyone runs after a vaccine. Who knows if the next commandment that we are going to share is 'a person has to get their vaccine by the sweat of their brow?

So, like this, it is a metastasis of capitalism wanting to eat all of us. And we need to sing, dance, and lift the sky, like people from different continents across the world; it's not just here in America, it's not just in South America, it's all over the planet. In Polynesia, there in those small islands of the Pacific, there in China, there in Asia, in Africa, in Northern Europe, there are people who are still clinging to the Earth and who live suckling the Earth. They don't take their bread with the sweat of their brow because they are not enemies of the Earth, they are children. The enemy must fight hard to get bread. The son asks for bread.

I'm asking for bread.

Pandemics time

I had thought that a rehearsal for my communication was very important so that I could infect people who watched or heard this speech, which will be virtual, which is another maneuver that we are undergoing, which is that of admitting that there is a screen between us and pretending that there is not. We pretend that we are having a date. We say, 'this is a live meeting'. So, in fact, the mediation that technology imposes on our meeting, prevents much of what we are complaining about, which is to let the Earth read our body and let our body read the Earth. We cannot be affected by what the Earth says if there is a screen between us and the Earth.

The screen that has persisted between us and the Earth is that screen established by a set of desires, values, ideologies; we continue to be exposed daily to this bombing, and with little resilience, with little capacity to produce from within our being the resilience necessary to not get sick. Because the essential question is this. If this ability that each one of us must produce life gets sick in each one of us, we will join a world that lies immersed in this pandemic misery, which produces more and more pandemic.

A dear writer here in Brazil, Conceição Evaristo, she said that most people, immersed in the pandemic, have not yet awakened that we are, in fact, being overcome by a pandemonium. In addition to the pandemic, the pandemonium, which admits the world is invaded by a mentality of negation, by a fascist mentality and by a praise of death, which is the very incarnation of necro-capitalism. That's when necro-capitalism is in minds and bodies, and people become zombies and are walking around, carrying necro-capitalism. In addition to a covid virus, the subject also integrates a necro-capitalist mentality. People are miserable but want to participate in necro-capitalism as a festival of achievement, of the delusion of achievement in a chaotic world, in a chaotic world.

SECTION 2 – DEBATING FREIRE'S IDEAS

This section is a collection of excerpts literally transcribed from the live debates that followed the lectures during the seminar *Paulo Freire Centennial: 7 Talks in Preparation for the Next 100 Years*, organized by Loughborough University London and Ubiqua, in March 2021[1].

These excerpts were organized under three titles that recover questions and answers recurrent during the debates.

Network Society: the digital gap; connectiveness; decolonizing technology; communication and media; fake news; algorithms; multimedia storytelling.

Social change: globalization; dialogue; building collectives; decolonizing social change; dealing with power relations; defining hope; meaning making; recognizing diversity.

Education: the objectives of education; pedagogies, structures, and practices.

---

1   Transcriptions provided by Fernanda Amaral; language review provided by Susan Weissert.

NETWORK SOCIETY

The Digital Gap

CLAUDIA MAGALLANES-BLANCO

I understand that the Network Society has, as [Manuel] Castells posits, structure and organization, a logic. But it's more than that. It is a logic of how the network society works. I do believe that we are constantly living in an online/offline world. We're not *only* online, not even in the pandemic, which has greatly increased our online presence. There are large numbers of people in this world who do not live online. This is not because they do not want to; it is because they cannot. They cannot have access. So, the digital gap *is* a reality. Looking at the network society, or understanding society as only a network society, is once again to look at one part of society that is in line with the paradigm of the neoliberal, colonial, capitalist world. I am not saying that it is not important or that it does not exist.

Therefore, I think that the debate, in denunciating or in support of the network society, must take place. We must discuss the network society in those terms to really have a critical perspective of it, to be able to question it, to subvert it and to use it in other ways. We believe it's not a matter of rejecting technology or rejecting what connectivity allows us to have. It is a matter of subverting it and using it for other purposes as well. For example, in indigenous communities there is the notion of one's own communication and one's appropriated communication. We need to be able to take this into other areas of our lives: those things that are true to us, to our hearts, to our practices, that allow us to be community and to be in community; as well as those things that we need to appropriate. But of course, we should have a critical perspective of those things we need to appropriate in order to appropriate them while subverting them.

MAYRÁ LIMA

We must consider what this concept of dialogue means for new life configurations, and mainly in the moment in which we live, when we need an online world in order to be in contact with other people. This is not the reality of the majority. This is a reality for a portion of the population that has access to the internet in Brazil, but not for the majority, despite smartphones which have limited internet packages. And most likely, other areas of Latin America have a similar reality. Even when there is connection, it isn't a very good connection. And the rural populations must be considered, even though most cities have much larger populations whose access is very precarious. Therefore, it is difficult to see 'connection' as a revolutionary aspect of new contacts or a certain globalization of contacts.

Are there transformations? There are. But there are also issues that require work. These issues are addressed through dialogue, the Freirean concept itself and within which we understand a formulation which is critical and focuses on social transformation. If you think about it, there are structural difficulties, elitist difficulties, platforms in which the monopoly has not been broken. On the contrary, this monopoly is further exacerbated when the world's largest companies (not only those of communication) act for profit and change the conformations of how people deal with life.

There, in the field of research, as well as in the establishment of the limits that arise from these technologies and that which stands as a concept of the network society, is that which [Manuel] Castells formulated, based on a vision that had mainly globalization as a horizon. We see how this can also be oppressive for many people around the world.

Connectiveness

ERIBERTO GUALINGA MONTALVO

For many of the original peoples, we are very far from all communication, far from the media. Only in recent years have we been able to reach communication spaces thanks to Instagram and this struggle for survival. At the same time, I am here communicating with you directly from the forest via satellite internet. I'm in my house with a leafy roof with internet access. Before, in order to communicate, we would have to leave and go to the city; all official communication, all those who spoke for us were through the mass media, speaking from their own point of view. Now this has been shifting a bit with the audiovisual work that we've carried on for several years now.

Despite this, there are people who are much further from the means of communication than we are; there are people who have no contact at all. There are people who listen to the radio, which in this case comes from the Capital Quito or Puyo, or from the big cities that bring the news. We want the original peoples to have their voices and to show their life missions, the importance of their territories, their struggle for development, so that they can make themselves known and survive as original peoples.

ANITA GURUMURTHY

What I am seeing are the ways in which in this 'shared grammar' seems to be homogenizing, universalizing on the social media network; well, I am not a poet, but I see a certain shared anger. At first, when given this opportunity to speak on humility I thought, 'Oh my God... maybe I should have been asked to speak on love. What do I say about humility?' But the more I thought about it, I thought 'maybe we live in times where we have the tools for true self-reflection, but we have allowed capitalism to appropriate those in very, very radical ways.'

I mean that because the way we relate to each other seems to bear the semblance of 'peerhood', of equality and the ability to be heard; but those don't exist. In some sense, I see that the search for an authentic self requires us to learn, I think, from the generations who are born 'digital'. And, what I see [there] is a tremendous degree of assertion, I think a very productive anger which is antithetical to humility in some ways. But they are extremely grounded ways by which, through a shared grammar of being interlinked in a global space, many of them are able to claim and define issues that pertain to their marginality. So, I feel very hopeful, because I don't think that being somewhat hybridized, caught in the nostalgia of my pre-digital life and perhaps the anxiety of one thinking about being cool enough and working enough.

I have increasingly come to accept that the fluidity between the virtual and the real has completely reconfigured my subject in relation to space. Even actors who are in the space of resistance perceive the virtual. They may or may not have the ability to frame it in this way, but I think that there is a certain seamlessness in the way in which social problems are defined across the real and virtual, or across the non-virtual and virtual, as well as how strategies and actions are planned across the virtual and the virtual. This includes people who may not really have the means to act online with 5-G networks and the best cameras and equipment.

Somehow, I think we see agents in society who are, let's say, polarizing society through their acts, inimical acts of virulent hate. Even they seem to be able to be most comfortable going onto a messaging app and sending things out. So, I see that it would be a losing battle if we were to become nostalgic. We cannot go back in time. And I think somewhere the architectures of technology recreate space and we really have to reconcile ourselves to that material fact, to that reality.

Decolonizing technology

LINJE MANYOZO

When I talk about media, let's say we talk about technology...Facebook, Twitter. Even before you put content there, the media are already biased because the person who designed this cellphone, the person who designed even the keyboard of a computer was not reading Marx, was not reading Gramsci. Thus, their mentality is already colonial at the time of creating a particular communication technology. So, I think we need people who are liberated, who are evolved in the designing of technologies that aim to serve people. The current technologies do not speak to the needs of the people. They are created with the idea of making money.

Communication and Media

LINJE MANYOZO

We should establish media and communication channels that are run by educational institutions. If we can find a better operational model that allows educational institutions to have control over the media, over communication instruments and channels, that will alleviate the problem. I haven't seen any successful business-oriented model that has been in the hands of communities for a long time.

When I was teaching in London, I used to go to Southeast London most of the time. There were some fantastic social enterprises, one of which was, if I'm not mistaken, the Greenwich Co-operative Development Agency. I used to ask questions of Claire Pritchard, the director of this particular place and other social enterprises at the time. I looked at it – it is a fantastic model! It does a little development work in the community; they have their own money, and they are doing fantastic work. And I asked, 'is it possible to have a media business that is run as a social enterprise?' Because that's when people will have ownership of the content, ownership of the editorial content and even ownership of the discussions and content that take place here. If we cannot resolve the business model conundrum, there is no way we can have media that is interested in the issues that people face.

JAMES DEANE

We are facing issues of a climate emergency. We are facing issues of the epidemic and obviously a great deal more. And pretty much all of the urgent issues we are confronting have to have some kind of collective action, have to be informed by approaches which are focused on people actually working together. And we have a communication system which is almost tailor-made, designed, to pitch people against each other, to actually foster misunderstanding, to drive people to see each other as 'other'. So, the talk of polarization is not only a polarization of opinion. It is polarization of identity in an age of cultural wars. And it seems that the source of political advantage is to find an in-group and an out-group, in other words, the complete opposite of a Freirean principle. There could not be a communication system at the moment which is better designed to be the inverse of what Freire was talking about. So, that's not encouraging; it's very depressing. The reason I'm so focused on issues of public interest media is that I actually think there's a crisis of trust in society (we've seen that crisis in the context of the pandemic), but also a crisis of debate, of having platforms for public debate in which people actually invest legitimacy and can actually engage in discussion with people who are different from them. And I think that's actually going to be a media challenge as well as a societal one.

The future of the development of democracy and society, of self-determination, has to be driven from within countries and it has to be driven on the foundation of an architecture of information and a communication system that work in the interests of the people of those countries, of the public interest. In the thirty or forty years I've been working in this field, there's never been a more depressing prospect than now, because there is no business model to pay for it. So, we have a combination of massive political corruption, which is finding it ever so easy to empty out the public media space. The democratic media space is now being occupied increasingly by authoritarian actors, and also by actors like China. There is a large amount of money coming from governments to enable that to happen. This is obviously not universal, but it is happening a lot. Because of the migration of online advertising to the big platforms, there is no business model capable of supporting independent journalism and the countries that are developing their own media and creative communication industries.

ERIBERTO GUALINGA MONTALVO

So, to whom did we make our voice heard? In my case, it was the young people from the universities. I also worked on a radio program for Catholic religious where the slogan was 'to give a voice to those who don't have a voice'. We started by teaching the Quechua language, teaching how to translate the news from Spanish into Quechua for all people in the Amazon who listen to this radio station and for all mestizos, say, who live in cities and also listen to this type of program in that language. So, through the radio and the audiovisual, we broadcast to these humble people and that was how our program was multiplied. Our films were taken to a film festival which made it widely known, and then it was carried out in different spaces. We also participate in meetings, forums, congresses of Native Peoples as well, always transmitting the message through audiovisual media. This is how we manage to make ourselves known, to reach the public and to bring our message.

The communication tool is very important in assuring that Indigenous Peoples can continue to live. What do we say when we have the voice when we hold the voice? What would we like to say? I would like to talk about the importance of the forest, of dreams, of traditional medicine and of nature for the survival of the world. Our means of communication, before, was the dream. We communicated through dreams before, through birds and through communication signals. But now, with modernity, we can communicate face to face, establish video conferences and discussions. We can do all this from the point of view of indigenous peoples.

Bring a message of life, bring a message of peace: That there are native peoples who are in all the forests of the world! That the forest in not uninhabited, it is not empty. There are people in the forests, people with different development ambitions from the people living in capitals. This is what we would like to say. There are many things to be taught, things that are not learned or taught in universities. For example, that a stone is alive, that a stone has energy. In school, one is taught that a stone is inert, that it has no life. But here, for native peoples, the jungle is alive, the forest is alive, the trees and stones and rivers are alive. They are the protective beings and that is the proposal that we have been working on for the past few years.

Fake News

FREI BETTO

I believe that fake news and denial are the symptoms that reflect the de-historization of time, a neoliberal proposal for us to believe in the permanence of capitalism and this belief in the permanence of capitalism is extremely strong. It is rare to find a critic outside of an intra-systemic logic. Many people believe that capitalism is reformable, and that if we file down the tiger's teeth it will become tame. I believe that the way to avoid this is to deepen the knowledge of historical facts. We need to show people that current phenomena result from a historical sequence, just as for each one of us, our personal life is a result of the story one has walked. Throughout our history, we've had several options and by embracing one of them, we've given up on many others. So, it is very important that we go back to extending the 'clothesline'.[1] If someone talks about neo-Nazism, we have to remember what Nazism meant. If anyone talks about the supremacy of the market, we have to remember that the stronger capitalism grows, the more poverty, misery and environmental destruction increase on our planet.

MAYRÁ LIMA

I believe that conflicts related to conservatism have to be understood and analyzed in a different way, because we are not dealing with debates that are totally rational. We are dealing with aggressiveness and denials. In the case of Brazil and the COVID-19 pandemic, in the first months of the year we have a daily average of 1,900 deaths, almost 2,000 people.[2] We are already the epicenter of the pandemic, surpassing the United States in terms of deaths. The President of the Republic told his population that this is a "mimicry". So, we are dealing with denial processes that, in my opinion, are not establishing conflicts that lead to social transformation. This is a mockery; this is denial. I believe we need to separate things, to analyze that the conflict arising from different ideological views isn't necessarily unhealthy within democratic frameworks of debate. Rather, that from the point of view of social transformations, conflict is fundamental for the working class as a whole to establish the same necessary transformations.

LINJE MANYOZO

I hear so much about this conflict: fake news, fake news, fake news. There was a time when I was in university watching CNN and BBC, and I said, 'What kind of news is this?' On the news about Africa, I couldn't recognize this Africa on the international news channels that I was watching. This wasn't because it was totally fake, but because of the kind of representations that were being made. Much literature and many studies have been written about how [people] are being represented, especially on the international media from the West. So, the first thing I want to say about fake news is that's been here for a long time. In fact, it was said in one of the responses by the Latin American Association of Bishops to the International Commission for the Studies of Communication Problems. in the 70s and 80s, that information should not be an article for merchandise, like a commercial enterprise. It should be aimed at liberating people. If that's our definition, our basis for defining what good journalism is all about, then I think we've had fake news for a long time.

And here we are in the 21st Century. The question we will be asking ourselves is 'what does objectivity mean anymore?', because in some of the models we are talking about, the state has absolute control over what goes on. What is objectivity anymore? And what is professionalism? So, even before we talk about fake news itself, the real issue is about values: the values of news, the values of content and editorial policies.

1   See a reference to Frei Betto's notion of 'clothesline' in his lecture, in Section 1 of this book.
2   Refers to the beginning of 2021.

Let me mention something that is very important. There is a quote from Marx in this beautiful book *The 18ᵗʰ Brumaire of Luis Bonaparte*, where he says that 'they cannot represent themselves, they must be represented'. He is talking about the conundrums of parliamentary democracy. Anybody has a right, in my opinion, to represent anybody. Anybody can talk about anybody, but one must have the moral authority to do that. You can talk about my mother if you understand who my mother is, if you take the initiative to know who she is. I can write about your parents; I can write about anybody. [But] we must put ourselves in a position to earn the right to talk about others, to theorize about others. I believe the process of theorization cannot be restricted to people who belong to certain social groups. It's a process in which anyone can be involved, but only if they have acquired a creative knowledge of the issues, of the people and of the places in question

Algorithms

ANITA GURUMURTHY

So, somebody said 'oh, my God! You know, in order to identify hate speech on Facebook, why are we using algorithms? They are the devil's own weapons, right?' But a lot of activists posit that we would be fighting a losing battle if we sought an authentic human process by which to recognize the millions and zillions of messages that appear on the screen every moment, dehumanizing peoples' existence or dehumanizing people with hate. So, you need algorithms to combat algorithms.

Another way to look at this -and sometimes at our own thinking and adapting for change- is: why do we think that algorithms do not have a human dimension? This is the reason given for why they always talk about bringing the human into the loop in AI studies, in the sense that it's possible to create algorithms with even a modicum of error or margin of error. Or, we could say that let's at least shortlist, because the machine is working at supersonic speed. Let's at least shortlist, on a daily basis, those offensive slurs that are posted against Dalit people, against black women, black people. Then of course we could do something about it. So, the questions are huge because the pace and the temporal and spatial scales of our existence demand that for every hegemonic package that is out there in the network, we also create equal spaces for indignation. I think that would be productive and regenerative. And we can only begin conversations when we are willing to accommodate people who simply do not have the vocabulary to be able to participate in these spaces.

Multimedia Storytelling

XAVIER CARBONELL

In today's world, as we know, young people are not particularly the best readers of history. So, we don't like large amounts of text; we don't like to spend five years to complete a program. We have been educated in this really fast world, but I have great faith in good stories, and I believe that deep down we have not renounced great stories. We are moved, we are interested, we are attracted by exceptional stories. We can see that in the movies or in today's visual culture. We are very visual beings right now. But if we use images or something to 'attract' alongside the text, to bring the reader in and to show what has been lost for all these years, imagine the amazing stories they can tell or they can read. You can awaken this lost affectivity, and this lost critical thought that seems to be gone from our readers - from our experienced readers, or users or students or commutators. So, *Unfold Nest!*[3] This book, this transmedia book, was precisely an attempt to attract many types of readers, through a life journey, a story that the reader can form by him/herself. I think that it works! I believe that if we show today's young people an amazing design on the website and an attractive story that can be recombine into many stories, we can bring back all of the adventure of reading these stories that we loved when we were children. It has a lot to do with re-discovering that curiosity and that spirit we had when we were kids.

---

3   See https://www.signis.net/news/events/22-05-2020/unfold-nest-a-signis-project-to-communicate-compassion.

SOCIAL CHANGE

Globalization

FREI BETTO

I do not think there is such a thing as globalization. What exits is 'global-colonization', that is, the imposition on the planet of liberal thinking that is predominant in Western Europe and the United Sates. That is to say, we live in a neo-colonial era. When I read yesterday that 80% of COVID-19 vaccines were bought by the richest countries and that all of Latin America, with its 600 million inhabitants, so far has bought only 5%, I see that we live in a

world where selfishness, 'dis-solidarity' are naturalized.

Dialogue

CLAUDIA MAGALLANES-BLANCO

I think, in using dialogue as a way to reach transformation, that conflict and dissent are key to the notion of dialogue of Freire. He is always looking, especially in *Pedagogy of the Oppressed*, at this polarization between the oppressed and the oppressor. And the whole point is to use dialogue as a way to reflect critically on the world, on the system and on the differences that put some people in the position of being oppressors and others in the position of being oppressed. So, I think conflict and dissent are at the forefront of understanding that there is a need for liberation. There is a need for emancipation, for transformation that is not only on the surface but is in the core of the system.

Of course, this is a constant even more so in our days, in the world in which we live. In Brazil, you have Bolsonaro. In Mexico we have AMLO and in other parts of the world you choose the character or the issue that brings people into different sides of one argument. But that's where the challenge lies: having a dialogue is not only having a conversation about the topic. Having a dialogue is much more profound because it is a way of really having a critical analysis of the reality that you can share on equal terms with someone else, even if that person is opposed to you. And that is a very difficult thing to achieve, of course. For example, in the case that I presented when this group of indigenous practitioners - communicators, facilitators, academic, indigenous, and non-indigenous - created during those two days of encounter, our conversation about the relationship with the government was intense.[1] We finally agreed that we had not reached an agreement and that there were opposing views because there were people who said 'we should not have to deal with the state in any way, shape or form; we should break all forms of relationship'. And there were other people said, 'but we need to create another relationship with the state and fight for our rights and everything'. So, it's not a matter of achieving consensus, but it is a matter of respecting the

---

1   See Claudia Magallanes-Blanco's lecture in Section 1 of this book.

differences and in spite of those differences, trying to build something that makes sense and that can help you move forward.

MAYRÁ LIMA

I would like to demystify this concept of conflict because it is diverse. I work with a concept of conflict that is very important, even for the class struggle. In this perspective, conflict is not necessarily a bad thing in principle, but it is an engine of class struggle, one of the engines of class struggle. In this sense, conflict is needed so that we can have spaces, constructions and syntheses that can be transformative. If there is no conflict, does that mean that everything is fine? Why are we going to fight? It is precisely in comprehending that there is oppression, that there are unequal realities, that there is exploitation in the most Marxist sense of the term, that we understand that there are conflicts to be built in society, so that we can dispute hegemonies in society and in the State.

We know that historically, in unequal societies such as Brazil and other Latin American countries, the understanding of political elites is very focused and close to [that of] economic elites, inhibiting popular debate from within the State. It is through understanding the methodological process of dialogue (which Paulo Freire identifies as a concept and improves as a method) that facilitates the establishment of conflicts. Because it's the conflict that makes us transform. It is the establishment of conflicts that makes us walk towards the necessary changes for a class; in this case, we are talking about the working class.

KARIN WILKINS

The issue of dialogue is really important. Thinking about Freire's work, it's not just dialogue between individuals, but the dialogue that we have that raises our sense of consciousness about the relationship of individual experience to the collective. It's about understanding that we are part of producing the structure, but also of being impacted by the structures that are within our world. And particularly when we are experiencing what might have seemed unimaginable in terms of Covid, in terms of climate change, in terms of the possibilities for a more just society, I think that dialogue becomes important. [It is important] that we teach understanding the importance of civility, but civility not as a way of silencing, but civility with justice.

XAVIER CARBONELL

There is no possibility of dialogue without love and compassion. And I say this because when we are discussing- in a classroom, a conversation or in a launch- the deepest and most complex parts of our spirits, you cannot wait for it to be simple. If no problems or no discussions or no conflicts emerge, it means there is nothing happening there. So, when someone comes out with a different notion, with a radically different proposition from the one you have, if you have no compassion, if you cannot give the other person or their opinion the dignity that they deserve, well, then dialogue is useless. And it's a selfish monologue that you're trying to prevail over other people's opinion. It makes no sense. So, love and compassion within the dialogue are the two basic components of how we can take these notions and give them an intellectual or theoretical shape.

COLIN CHASI

I think that questioning, questioning with indignation, the world in which we live is a fundamentally important thing. I would like to talk finally of the ideas with which we've grappled today, ideas having to do with humility. We've encountered the idea that humility involves recognizing our limitations. I would also say that recognizing all of our possibilities is also part of humility. To only recognize your limitations is perhaps some kind of masochism, right? Or at least to be perhaps entrapped within a particular kind of masochism. You must also recognize your possibilities. And the negotiation of these things is the journey of human beauty. And, in many ways, that is the journey of humility. It's an incomplete answer, but I certainly think that indignation is absolutely indispensable, absolutely unavoidable in the face of the structural and other forms of violence and injustice in which we find ourselves. Without that, we cannot remake the world.

Building Collectives

MAYRÁ LIMA

Many here asked 'How do you manage to escape interdictions?', 'How do you dialogue with teachers?', 'How do you do this?', 'How do you do that?' I think that there is no other answer than to find, in popular organizations, a capacity for dialogue with those sectors. It doesn't' seem to me that they will be isolated, or that an individual alone will be able to establish the necessary transformation. It seems to me that the aspects of solidarity and collectivity are central to any mechanism and to any process of overcoming difficulties. This includes the global situation of an extremely conservative extreme right that is consolidated in several countries. So, it all seems to me to go against, to go the other way around, neoliberal perspectives.

We have a project that is political, that is economic, that does not serve us. And if it doesn't suit us, then we have the basic fundament of any organization: to correctly analyze it in order to establish the necessary tactics to overcome it. And it seems to me that only with mechanisms of dialogue, solidarity and collectivity will we have more adequate responses around the world.

LINJE MANYOZO

There is an aspect of Freire which has been controversial for a long time, even when I was a student. In *Pedagogy of the Oppressed*, Freire talks about the oppressed having the moral, political, and historical responsibility to liberate themselves and of course, to liberate the oppressors as well. Some of us come from Africa, where we had secular colonization, and especially in South Africa, where we had apartheid for a long time. For us, it might seem a huge burden to think of your oppressor as well; to consider that they deserve to be liberated after enjoying all the privileges of colonization and the privileges of power.

But I think that Freire meant that if the oppressed are victorious, and if through the revolution they are able to empower or have overcome certain issues, then if they victimize other people or certain groups of people, then those people become the oppressed and the cycle of revolution goes on, and on, and on.

AILTON KRENAK

The poet Carlos Drummond de Andrade said that the man, a small animal, gets tired of the Earth, sick of the Earth. And then he invents a rocket to go into space. *We* need to embrace the Earth. If we don't hug the Earth, we're going to have an inverse experience of the law of gravity. When school children are told that an apple fell on Newton's head, the kids don't know whether they're thinking of Newton or of eating the apple. Depending on where you tell a story like this, kids will go crazy wanting an apple, because there are many places in the world that don't have apples. Then the children are thinking: 'Wow! I want to eat an apple!'. We need to hug the Earth, otherwise what Newton learned with the apple falling on his head will happen with the sky falling on *our* heads. And the sky is much heavier than an apple.

Decolonizing Social Change

LINJE MANYOZO

Paulo Freire was a very radical man, really radical. And I think some of his ideas have been taken captive, have been depoliticized, especially by international development organizations; they claim to do his work, but they are actually contributing to the oppression that is going on in many, many countries. Instead of dealing with the root causes of marginalization and inequality, they are doing charity.

In the paper that Thomas Tufte and Ana Suzina[2] have written, they talk about this other kind of empathy that is almost a kind of challenge. And in my opinion, that is what a lot of international development organizations are doing. They are becoming part of the development industry, which is very oppressive, very colonial and is not interested in rooting out the key sources of under-development and inequality. That's why you never hear of an organization closing shop and saying 'No, we have achieved our objectives'. They continue asking for more funding, claiming to be doing participatory work, constructive work. But it's not Freire!

2　See complete reference in the Introduction.

Dealing with Power Relations

JAMES DEANE

Regarding the talk on authoritarianism, last week a report came out from the V-Dem Institute in Stockholm. Every year it does a democracy report and it's very good. For two or three years now, they have been pointing to how democracy has actually become what has been a well-established 'authoritarian playbook' by authoritarians and autocrats all over the world. I just pulled it up here: 'The Playbook of "wannabe" dictators seems to have been shared widely among leaders in (former) democracies. First, seek to restrict and control the media while curbing academia and civil society. Then couple these with disrespect for political opponents to feed polarization while using the machinery of the government to spread disinformation. Only when you have come far enough on these fronts, is it time for an attack on democracy's core: elections and other formal institutions.' I think that's exactly right. The root to power, to the exercise of power, to the exercise of authoritarian power is to control the means of communication - but not in the way of the old propagandistic Soviet model, or simply by dictating your own narrative and controlling everything, but by seeding so much confusion. And I think this is Putin's playbook. No one knows what to trust, no one knows what to believe and effectively, you can pitch everyone against each other. You can get one group of people to hate other groups of people. We have to find a solution to that and again, I think that Freire is relevant here. I think that it's extremely difficult to find solutions to it, but it's very difficult to see where human progress can be advanced in the future if the information and communication model is effectively ... provides infrastructure for the planet, so we have to find solutions to this.

BENJAMIN FERRON

How do we create an ecology of knowledge, which will consist of dialogue and hope? I think this is a tough question. It's related to the difficulties I would have answering politically to the question 'what is my position as a citizen?'. I don't believe, as a sociologist, that speeches, words, have intrinsic power by themselves. Sociological observation shows that the power of words is intimately linked with the social or institutional position of who is speaking and who is listening, or what we call a field of production of speeches and a field of receptions. So, as a teacher in a French public university, my voice is intimately linked with my position as a functionary of the state and it gives a kind of legitimacy to what I say, legitimacy I wouldn't have on saying the very same things in an alternative university with no institutional recognition. On the other hand, at the same time, I worked a lot on the political experiences such as the Zapatistas in Mexico, who fought precisely to create alternative institutions from the unjust state, the Mexican state. And we can see that almost thirty years later, they created alternative institutions in terms of health, in terms of education and agricultural production, etc. So, you can see that you are not necessarily a prisoner of the existing institutional order, which gives force or weakness to your voice. One of the political messages I would put forth would be to think about what kind of institutional arrangement would be appropriate to give legitimacy to dominated voices. There are many ways to do it. Even as I said before, in such alternative institutions you have to be careful with the fact that relationships of domination do not magically disappear when, in good will, you create an egalitarian space to emancipate the dominated. You have to think about the way domination is a very vicious snake which reproduces itself exactly where you think you have made it disappear.

ERIBERTO GUALINGA MONTALVO

How to build hope? [We build hope] by listening to us, listening to us, to ourselves, knowing ourselves, because there are different peoples. It is not because we are small that we cannot be heard. We are listened to within universities, within cities, in large institutes. So, I think now is the time to listen to indigenous peoples, to listen to the voice of nature. Because the world is changing. The Amazon is disappearing more and more; there are more and more extractive interests and huge projects. And I believe that this is the time to turn our vision, our view, to the original peoples, to look at the indigenous people because we have learned a lot from you. We have also been to universities, but at the same time, we also want to hear the voice of the indigenous people so that we can get to know each other, so that we can look at each other face to face. Thus, we can talk and discuss about the future, about life expectancy, about the future of the world, the future of the original peoples…about our lives, our children. I believe this is the time to consider the little ones too.

There are large spaces, such as the Conference of the Parties that is organized around the world, and native peoples are not taken into account. There are other side events involving indigenous people, which are organized to talk to indigenous peoples around the world. However, we do not participate in the spaces where the presidents of the world meet. The voices of native peoples are not heard in these spaces, are not heard in these official spaces, so how are we going to be known? Therefore, there should be pressure from all over the world, from universities, institutions, environmental organizations, etc. Everyone must move so that these spaces are also open to native peoples so that we can be heard in official spaces, where the presidents of the world are.

COLIN CHASI

In the context of Africa, one of the more interesting recent explorations (of power relations) is in a book entitled *Globalectics* by Ngugi wa Thiong'o. In *Globalectics*, Ngugi looks at the African attempt to decolonize ourselves, and he recognizes the fact that to be African is to be fundamentally always cosmopolitan. It is always to be yes, African, in a wide range of ways that are deeply problematic. These ways have deep roots, deep traditions, that must be understood in a particular moment of time and reference particular possible futures, always in these deeply cosmopolitan ways. [Ngugi] suggests that we recognize that we cannot try to be decolonized by somehow returning to some kind of pure pre-colonial pristine form that one might try and theorize or imagine. The decolonial possibilities really are possibilities that involve a deep humility, allowing us to embrace those aspects of others that will become part of the world that we co-inhabit with them. And if we can embrace that humility with the possibility of working with love, we are able to redesign how we live. And this is the source of flourishing. It is something that is deeply rooted in this idea of altruism.

ANITA GURUMURTHY

I think resistance is always from within, in a sense that it is resistance in relation to a particular power relationship. So then, the challenge for resistance and action is really: is subversion enough? Is it enough to produce a meme on Instagram to look at something that might be terribly racist and patriarchal, or do you need to create an alternative space itself? And I think that the creation of that alternative space, or a space with a different normative axis, is really the most crucial question. It is at the same time both an international and global question as it is a national and subnational question. And I think that because our time-space configurations are really very different now, and everything happens at a very rapid pace, there is a most urgent need for public reasoning that can grapple with creating or redeeming privatized public architectures of democracy and expression. And the more the developing countries and people who are on the margins are worried that this is not really about public policy issue, that this is not really about global norms setting, I think the more we should be convinced that we are being misled. And I believe that in those spaces it's really important to come out with that pride, which is the other side of humility, and to assert that resistance and action do call for completely reclaiming public space.

Defining Hope

BENJAMIN FERRON

This depends on the way you define hope, because today you can have three main definitions of hope that are circulating in contemporary society. The first I would call the 'psychological' definition, which is defining hope as a state of mind. For example, being optimistic has the psychological aspect of seeing light in the darkness. I think that today, in capitalist societies, this psychological imperative to stop being pessimistic and to see the good side of life can easily functions as an ideology culture, serving to maintain the social, economic, and political status quo. We see that, for example, in the personal development industry, where they say, 'you should aim at changing yourself before aiming at changing the world.' This is a very bad interpretation of what Gandhi said, because he was promoting collective action and not only action directed toward oneself.

The second definition of hope would be a political definition, meaning to collectively produce a moral and political imperative such as 'giving hope to the hopeless.' I think that's something common to political-religious enterprises that aim to overcome fatalism and to raise the consciousness of the possibility of changing the unjust rules of the social game. That's what sociologist Max Weber calls the enterprise of manipulation of the salvation gods. I think that kind of political definition is found in in Christianity, as well as in Marxism or in the ideology of meritocracy of the French educational system.

Today, I want to call your attention to a more sociological definition of hope, meaning the feeling produced by the incorporation of social structures. This means, as [Pierre] Bourdieu analyzed it, when studying the sub-proletarian workers in Algeria or the French educational system, the mismatch between subjective aspiration (what one thinks is possible) and objective chances (what is statistically possible). I think this mismatch is a sociological exception rather than the social rule.

Hope is an exception in the sense that Paulo Freire defines hope. In general, class habits of people favor an adjustment between subjective hopes and objective possibly. We generally love what we can do, what we can have. So, I think on the other hand that in some situations, in some specific adjustment between people and social structure, the feeling of hope is growing. And I think that's the kind of situation that permits possible action to transform the social order.

Meaning Making

FREI BETTO

To work with the masses, the people who pass by, here in Brazil and in many countries, who spend long hours on public transport to and from work, there are two very efficient resources.

First, the religious. Contrary to all intellectual predictions, the Enlightenment did not make religiosity disappear in humanity. This will last as long as there is poverty, that is, religion is the most comprehensive system of meaning that has ever been created by human beings. Every human being seeks a system of meaning on which to imprint its existence. What really makes a person happy is the meaning s/he gives to their existence. It is not wealth; it is not possessions or titles. It is the meaning which is the main reason. And since most people on the planet are poor or are well off, they find in religion this one-way system that answers all sorts of questions. No other system of meaning is as comprehensive as religion. And, in many countries, as in all of Latin America, with the exception of Uruguay, the cultural base of the people is viscerally religious. And in Latin America, if you ask a simpler person, a fisherman, a peasant a maid 'what do you think about life? what do you think about the future?', surely, they will give an answer woven within religious category. So, valuing the religion of ordinary people is extremely important to be able to motivate them to join popular groups.

But there is another resource: entertainment. All of us, without exception, from the poorest to the richest, travel in two spheres. In the sphere of need, we need to work, to earn a salary to support the family, to pay for house and transport, to be healthy. This is the sphere of need, which greatly absorbs us. But there is another essential sphere, that of gratuity. There are times when we need to turn on the television and watch a really silly movie. There are times we want to go to the cinema, the theater, watch a song festival or a party, you know? It is essential to be free. If you want to have a picnic with the family, go to a park. One cannot live all the time immersed in the sphere of necessity. So, a good way to work with these busy people on a day-to-day basis is through entertainment.

I always say, if you want to do 'popular' work, tell me what you like to do. 'Oh, I love playing the guitar'. So, go to the favela and organize a group around music. 'I like drawing a lot'; then organize a drawing workshop, a cooking workshop. This is the bait, the hook with which we will approach the cooking, guitar or theatre class, or the class on film history: the method of Paulo Freire. The people move from this lively niche to awareness, and then to a more conscious mobilization. That is what I see in the history of all of this popular work in Brazil and Latin America, because I have also worked with popular education in many [other] countries, such as Nicaragua and Cuba.

Recognizing Diversity

AILTON KRENAK

Paulo Freire insisted on the idea that you use straw, clay, and water, and you make a brick. You could build a building with this material. But first, it emerges from an awareness of where you are. If you are not aware of where you are, it is very unlikely that you will develop an ability to recognize the other, in the sense of 'otherness'; to respect the existence of the other not as a competition, but as a stimulus to diversity. The other is a confirmation of diversity, not of equality. When I want equality with the other, I want to swallow the other, absorb the other. When I admire the sense of 'otherness', I see the other and admire the difference. The more difference can be observed, the more diversity will be produced; and equality will be repelled because equality is the infinite reproduction of an unsustainable thing.

The first observation about our intrinsic diversity is that it is not our choice. We do not choose to be different. We are different because we are nature and nature just produce difference: It's wonderful! Monoculture produces equality. When there is a plague on a large plantation, everything dies. Coffee dies, sugarcane plantations die. And if Brazilian agribusiness is attacked by a pest, the capitalist fanfare that happens here in the soybean monoculture will die of shame. This is because if there is a plague, every soybean dies because they are all the same. If we had thousands of types of seeds, as Vandana Shiva says, it could happen that some of them will die as a result of a plague, but others will live. And life does that to us. The diversity of life produces life and monoculture produces death. It is obvious.

EDUCATION

The Objectives of Education

FREI BETTO

In order to decolonize education, we must first avoid education being merely a training to prepare skilled labor for the market. So, the role of education is not to qualify people for the market. The role of education, in the first place, is to make us happy from a personal point of view. And, from a social point of view, make us citizens, social, political, economic protagonists, endowed with critical conscience. It is not easy, because as the old Marx said, the ideology that prevails in a society is the ideology of the class that dominates that society.

MAYRÁ LIMA

When you contrast happiness and educational processes and people's real lives, that is, people's concrete lives, I don't think I have any response than to point to the experiences of popular organizations seen around the world. These are potential spaces for the establishment of criticisms that are so necessary not only to establish syntheses but also for the transformation of reality.

Happiness is something individual, yes, but we live in society, and it also depends on some structure and what you set as a parameter for happiness. Happiness is having had a good education, having had a good job. But what are the social structures with which I live that can facilitate these paths for me? Or am I alone in the world wherever I am?

XAVIER CARBONELL

It takes a lot to create the conditions and background in the structure of a career or a university to allow this kind of experience. Usually, people in the cupola of power of a university are not prepared to accept that learning cannot be totally programmed. It has a lot to do not only with the minds of the students, but also with their own lives. It takes a lot to convince a professor or an educational system that not everything can be predicted, not everything can be foreseen. And perhaps there could be a way to talk about the essence of how the experience of different educational systems ought to inform the conservative tendencies that we see today.

I have had conversations and talks with my friends from very different backgrounds, and I have noted that, of course, it's natural for a conservative government or for a conservative party to restructure education according to their own interest and principles. But we must not think that in other kinds of countries or perhaps socialist countries, like Cuba or others in Latin America, that it works differently. There is a tendency to be conservative that doesn't depend on ideology.

We can see today that many governments attempt to restructure education to create a kind of citizen that abandons every critical thought. So, it can be seen not only in countries with conservative governments, but also in 'third world' countries. And in all education right now there is an effort to take back the critical components in our education, to forbid the kind of programs that, in their complexities, seem to be impossible or impractical, or useless for today's world. And the thought of such programs is always a reason to laugh for some department heads in some universities; they would not allow us to study on their properties. Perhaps in small countries it can be even clearer: even if there is no private education or all education is controlled by one power, it can be seen clearly how today's governments are trying to redirect education to their own ideology. They are trying to plant a seed for the future. We are not seeing the impact of this right now, but we can see how difficult it will be to have a critical student or a compassionate student, or a critical or compassionate communicator in the future. So, this is why programs like the *Laudato Si'* Certificate in Compassion in Social Communication[1] are so necessary in today's world, in order to implement and encourage those who are working on these initiatives.

ERIBERTO GUALINGA MONTALVO

I think this is the way for the world to continue: to go back to the roots, make a profound change in our lives and go back to the beginning without destroying nature. And I think this is also how we should teach in educational institutions, loving nature for example. Students, children should be taught not only about technology, but also how to help through technology. We should teach how to find mechanisms to, for example, seek, study, and find alternative energy sources, so that we can continue without relying exclusively on oil and mineral energy sources. I think this is a fundamental issue in the educational field, both in schools and in universities, colleges, etc. 'They' discovered oil; this is science, but science also needs to pay attention to what is traditional, to the original peoples. I think this is the path that we should follow.

COLIN CHASI

I'm grappling with the challenge of doing some work for our university, where we are asking the question, 'how can we be more impactful?'. And in our context, part of the challenge is that universities that have operated to a great extent as ivory towers have attempted to mimic in so many ways European and Western-based universities. We've addressed problems, challenges that are not necessarily problems, challenges that are faced within the communities in which we find ourselves. I've therefore begun to be deeply interested in work that talks about how we can re-establish the university as a central hub within the cities within which it is found. This reconceptualization of the University, of its activities within the communities, within particular cities and so on can enable us to once again belong in the places where we find ourselves.

---

1   See Xavier Carbonell's lecture in Section 1 of this book.

We need to think about some methods with which we can engage with these communities in which and with whom we find ourselves living. In our case, at the University of the Free State, we have established an office that facilitates these interactions. We fear that the exploitative nature of the universities that we have established can lead to relations with communities that are deeply destructive. We need to somehow find a way to learn best practices and to take ourselves as actors that need to be treated at once with suspicion, but also with love, with generosity. And we need to recognize that the communities have been feeding us, supplying us with insights, with problems, with challenges and so on. It's difficult to give a comprehensive answer but in short, what we require is a complete rethinking of what the university is. We need to reformulate the university within the communities where we find ourselves. And this is perhaps, in my view, the greatest task that faces us as universities, certainly in South Africa.

ANITA GURUMURTHY

We are coming from India, and we understand the public university as a critical space, not only for intellectual debate, but also for the very important framings of political citizenship. I do think that the loss of that space or the erosion of that space flags a lot of concern. And this is slightly different from the way in which processes of legitimation operate where I work, in the publishing world. What is valued is that which can be measured. What is valued is what could be quantified. So, you're approaching knowledge itself from a different starting point, which finds financial as well as ideological affirmation in the way capitalism works. So, I think that there are innumerable experiments in India where direct participation with communities exists in university spaces. But how, then, does that become part of what becomes the rubric of democracy? It is the political gap that becomes vital to the way agenda setting takes place.

LINJE MANYOZO

Now, why is education very important? You know, a lot of people graduate, and they have no clear understanding of the issues we face in today's world. Yes, they have the knowledge; they have the skills to perform specific duties. But a number of years ago, after the financial crisis in 2007, a group of students at Manchester University released what is called CRESC economic society. It was, I think, a kind of manifesto. But in that document, they said that the educational system, especially in the West, has failed students. It had given preference to western perspectives over perspectives from other parts of the world. Most of the time, when a student graduates from a western university, but even from a university from the Global South, they only see the world from a set of linear perspectives; they don't have much of a universal perspective. I think it's a teacher's responsibility. I'm glad Loughborough University is involved in these debates.

We have the moral responsibility to provide alternative perspectives, alternative theories to our students so that they have a critical understanding of the issues. Even the topic of development; we talk about development as if it were not problematic. Development is a very colonial concept because it has some obligations, some baggage that comes with it. What is it that people want on the ground? It'll not necessarily be development as it's calibrated in the documents by international development organizations. So, I think Freire paid so much attention to education because he knew that revolution requires educated people, liberated people, people who really understand what the struggle is all about. And I think a lot of educational institutions and international development organizations are continuing with the tradition of oppressing and denying students the opportunity to understand this alternative perspective.

AILTON KRENAK

Most likely UNESCO and other bodies, as well as the World Health Organization were called upon to assume their responsibility since it is a part of the globalization game. So, each of these players, each of these globalization players who make a lot of money in this global casino, will be socially and morally summoned to say what will happen to education after the pandemic. UNESCO cannot pretend to be dead. UNESCO didn't die of Covid: this will be our next campaign. Let's run a campaign saying 'UNESCO Lives', for UNESCO to stand up and say what will happen to the public education system on the planet. How will the pedagogical vaccine be?

So, we're going to say 'look, let's start now to get supplies to produce a pedagogical vaccine'. We're going to have to take care of our lives in a world shocked by the mortality of the pandemic, which doesn't end this year or next year. And everyone who is aware knows that after we've vaccinated everyone on the planet, we should, yes, have a quarantine. After we vaccinate everyone, everyone on the planet. When the WHO says, 'everyone in the world, except those who refused and gave some justification mechanism for not getting the vaccine, everyone else did'. Then we'll say: so now let's do a quarantine. Then it'll be like 40 days around the world without doing anything, while we think about what education will be like in the future.

Pedagogies, structure, practices

FREI BETTO

The structure of schools, as it exists today, was shaped to favor banking education. Just look at the format of a classroom, where students are as an assistant audience, sitting in their chairs, while the teacher occupies a higher platform where his desk and chair are. It is as if s/he were the holder of all knowledge and will deal with the blank slate of culture. But it is necessary, yes, to introduce Paulo Freire into the schools; I would even say that sometimes without talking about Paulo Freire, so as not to draw too much attention to his name. Doing as Pope Francis acts in relation to capitalism: in all the documents, he harshly criticizes capitalism, but in none of them does the word 'capitalism' appear, because there are words that create emotional blocks. So, wherever it is possible to talk about Paulo Freire without using his name, let's do it like this. But where this is not possible, let us adopt the most important thing, which is Paulo Freire's method.

In fact, in formal education, I don't know of any experience that serves as a reference for applying Paulo Freire's method. There are schools where one or another teacher uses the method, but the institution as a whole does not. Even in Cuba, when I started my work with popular education in the early 80s, Cubans said 'here, everything is popular education.' It was not. It was an excessively banking education, not least because of the Soviet influence.

So, in Latin America what predominates from Paulo Freire comes from social movements, NGO's and now identity movements. In Cuba, the Martin Luther King Center was created, an important institution of popular education. For a long time, it was the only NGO admitted in the country, which I had helped to found and which has already been operating for thirty years. And the introduction of the Paulo Freire method was another revolution within the revolution, in the sense of breaking this banking education out of socialism. I would even say that sometimes it was stronger than within capitalism because of the idea that everyone who is born in a socialist country is supposed to be ontologically socialist, and it doesn't happen like that.

So, in fact, the experience of solidarity, the experience of love is an experience that results from the unfolding caused by education. The education is what unfolds us to love or not, to love, to have solidarity, empathy, in short, all those virtues that should be natural to human beings.

KARIN WILKINS

I think that it is an interesting and important task to try and understand how we take the central principles in Freire and apply them in a world that has perhaps a different, or differently enabled power structures, with digital platforms. And then, what does that mean for education? So, we are thinking about the architecture of education. In part, it's about curricula and decolonizing curricula, which may have to do with the content, you know, what we assign to students. But it can also have to do with what kinds of academic programs we create: certificates, majors, and minors. I also think it's important to think about what we enable in that architecture, what possibilities we can create for students to learn from each other. For students who are privileged enough to get to universities, such as the one in which I work, I think it's important to them to have time off-campus, whether it's off-campus locally or abroad, or just in another city in the United States. I think that is a part of enabling an architecture of experience and possibility. That also means thinking through our communities locally and globally and the ways in which that is important to that architecture of education.

ERIBERTO GUALINGA MONTALVO

When I finished my first film, called *I Am the Defender of the Forest*, I had only worked as an assistant on a few videos before taking my audiovisual course. And this film was made because they were going to militarize my territory, claiming that we were terrorists because, at the time, we were opposed to an oil extraction company. I went to the Catholic University of Ecuador and showed my film before I finished it. I showed the film and the young people liked it, and asked: 'What is happening here in Ecuador? Where are the Sarayaku people?' That's when I realized that universities were not studying the reality of native peoples. Universities, students among Ecuadorians – we didn't know each other as people of a same country. And these young people formed movements to bring a voice in favor of the people of Sarayaku where I am from. And that's how we started this great fight in defense of my people and of nature.

COLIN CHASI

I think it is a very difficult question about how to move beyond mechanical teaching. We need to rethink the university as such. I've been looking at the problem of assessments within the university, assessments as things that are actually closing the door to learning. Now, Freire teaches quite the opposite: questioning should open the door to learning. This is Freire. We go back to Socrates, the maieutic method and so on. In our contexts, we find that students come in week 2, week 3. They begin to write assignments in a fourteen-week block and write up to 40 assessments. Significant assignments. Right. So that's three, four assessments a week. There is a good deal of evidence, once one starts to examine how such how such mechanical approaches to assessments can be regressive, that this can cause unintended outcomes where students abilities to peak in their performances are actually harmed. So, students suffered from being given this incredible amount of work that is unsustainable.

In our case, students often come into the university relatively poorly equipped and then are heavily burdened by these assessments. So, assessments become the source of negative outcomes as opposed to becoming the germ, the route for insights, and instead of questioning and opening doors to new insights, they become something that closes them. Now we need to rethink the whole way in which we assess students. A Freirean set of insights into the role of questioning could be an interesting way to begin to rethink such an important practice. But at the moment we are stuck in a failing, mechanized way of thinking about how a university should work. The role, for example, of assessments. We could engage in that sort of a discussion about many, many other aspects of how we engage in teaching and learning. But what we need to do in the first instance is to have the courage, the humility to rethink what we have been given, what we have received. And I think that's a profoundly decolonial task.

AILTON KRENAK

All of these ethnic groups that were mentioned in addition to the Krenak have their own, let's say, pedagogies, their ways of forming mentalities, people. And they have the common characteristic, which is to form collective subjects. None of these educational experiences constitute the subject in the sense of the ego. Nobody talks to the ego; people like to talk to each other. And this institutes collectives. It's as if you lay down in a valley, and instead of hearing a voice answering you, you hear the landscape answering. It is collective; it is not individual.

The approach to education that is done in the public system and even in the universal system of education is aimed at the individual, the subject. In the cultures of native peoples, this subject is collective. So, it's as if when you address someone, you are sending out a plural signal to everyone, including non-humans, pro-humans, and humans. It's not anthropocentric language. It's a language that wants to talk to nature. Really! They [indigenous children from Krenak people] make sounds that are birds, sounds that are the wind. They make sounds that are what we conventionally call nature. Children grow up listening to the wind speak. Children grow up listening to the words of rain birds, and they learn this vocabulary and share. We have a common perspective. We have a diversity of ways to apply that perspective. Perhaps this is what Eduardo Viveiros de Castro calls 'Amerindian perspectivism'. So, it is not contained in a list of ethnicities, but in Amerindian. The native peoples of the continent, *Abya Yala*. They have not yet created this abstraction as an individual. That amazing individual that the Greeks seeded, and the rest of the world cultivates: The Ego.

We are talking about education before we should be concerned about teaching children to read and write. I am talking of children and not adults. We should consider the possibility of awakening the contact of children in early childhood to the experience of metamorphosis, the experience of transformation and the experience of this kind of transfiguration in which these beings could experience the fantastic dance of life. Then bring knowledge later, only in the applied sense. If I'm going to be a doctor, then I am going to study something so I can be a 'healer'. If I'm going to be an architect, I'm going to get more and more involved with the experience of materials with which I'm going to build our shelters, our structures. But we are not going to fill a child with information as if s/he were a computer chip, 99% of useless information that will only harm h/her spirit. S/he will be full of garbage, and we haven't found a way to recycle this mental garbage yet. Only psychiatrists want to resolve this but then everyone will have to go to psychiatrist after finishing school So, we have to stop putting garbage in children's heads. For adults: when approaching an adult from this perspective, I think we should consider Davi Kopenawa Yanomami's pedagogy which is to lie down on the ground and wait for the Earth to talk to you.

SECTION 3 – FREIRE FROM THE PERSPECTIVE OF YOUNG SCHOLARS

We asked six young doctoral students, with past or current experience in grassroots work, to write about their perspectives regarding the place and role of Freire's thoughts to think the world today, associating their reflections with their own experience and local challenges they face and observe in their communities or countries. They all have attended the cycle *Paulo Freire Centennial: 7 Talks in Preparation for the Next 100 Years*, in March 2021. This section gathers their reflections[1].

---

1   Language review provided by Susan Weissert.

RE-THINKING COMMUNICATION AS A POLITICAL TOOL WITH CRITICAL OPTIMISM

FANIA SÁNCHEZ DE LA VEGA GONZÁLEZ

At the end of 2019, information and communication technological devices (nICTs[1]) connected to the internet were already quite common on a day-to-day basis, mediating social interactions in private and public spaces. Just a couple of months after the global lockdown was implemented in response to the Covid-19 pandemic, education centers, workplaces, governments, the market, the health system, as well as both big and small organizations around the world became aware of the urgent need to stay connected. Actors of all kinds across the world needed to continue their work using any electronic device or media available: smartphones, personal laptops, smart TVs, electronic tablets, or similar tools, all linked to the internet by some platform, web site, app or social media. These technologies rapidly became great tools that allowed remote human exchange and contributed to reducing the risk of contagion. The accelerated digital migration prompted by the pandemic came up as a new human-technological evolution, triggering major and -apparently- irreversible social effects such as the fact that online reality is now as important as offline reality.

If we go back several months, even before the public health emergency, we could remember multiple social conflicts and protests that sprang up around the world, many of which were broadcast in different mass and independent media. But upon entering quarantine, the world seemed to sink into an unprecedented limbo, where social problems remained unresolved: inequities, injustices, rising crises, new exclusions and increasing dehumanizing conflicts. In other words, in less than two years the global society created more oppressed people under new forms of oppression.

Parallel to the above, digitality also devised other ways of existing in the world, allowing other human interactions to emerge; ways of relating that were difficult to imagine in the past, are possible now. Thanks to this, 856 people from 490 cities around the world could listen and participate in a virtual event to think about five Freirean concepts applied to the field of communication on the occasion of the 100 years of Paulo Freire's birth[2].

At the beginning of the series of the 7 talks, I was wondering to what degree Freire's epistemology has had general, large-scale, or paradigmatic influence on the practice of Communication? James Deane's talk was one of the most revealing about this for me. He narrated his experience as a media and communication practitioner throughout four decades of work, ensuring that people have access to relevant information for them that can affect their lives.[3] His story provided evidence about how Freirean epistemology has influenced a number

---

1   The acronym nICTs refers to new Information and Technology Technologies such as mobile devices, platforms, web services, and social media networks connected through internet.
2   https://www.paulofreirecentennial.org/principal-in/.
3   *James Deane, 'Paulo Freire and Empathy and its implications for media and communication*

of important organizations in the field of communication including the BBC Media Action, the International Fund for Public Interest Media, Earthscan and Panos, where dialogue became the key to empower those most affected by an issue[4].

Deane recalled how 'in the early years of these [social media] platforms there was immense excitement about the potential to translate these principles into reality at huge scale by providing unprecedented fresh access to amplify previously marginalized voices and provide new opportunities to connect and organize.'[5] This story reminded me of the naive optimism in technology about which I was warned by my mentors when I presented my master's research advances about how the new information and communication technology (nICTs) had become a tool for the organization and advocacy of the undocumented youth immigrant movement in the U.S. in the last two decades.

Since then, I became more cautious when analyzing social movements that throughout 2020-2021 utilized new ICTs as technopolitical tools. By creating and recreating new digital protest strategies, occupying virtual spaces now, writing their own agendas, self-representing in their own media channels and telling their own stories, they make the prophecy of free, democratic, collective, and liberating media become true.

As referred by Deane[6], I like to believe that ICTs can allow the person 'to come out of silence, pronounce their own world and through the knowledge generated by the word, fully develop as a human being based on free, revealing, and creative dialogue.'[7]

On the other hand, as Deane mentioned, 'the business model for independent journalism is broken'[8] especially in countries where the political and market powers invest greatly in controlling the media. So, although the pandemic seemed to announce the crisis of neoliberal capitalism, it managed to reinvent itself. But how? As Midas who could turn everything he touched into gold, digital communication controlled by the big corporations seems to turn any social resistance and grassroots activism into a marketing plan, key performance indicators (KPI's), followers and views, data analytics, *entrepreneurship*, etc.

Marketing has been reaching sociopolitical movements by distracting them with more and newer digital and social media platforms. These platforms are built under the logic of consumption, forcing movements to think about users, buyers, and donors instead of people. In addition, they are made to use the most popular or latest app and their reductionist formats to promote the culture of liking and viralization, in a meaningless universal language. All of this occurs by taking the complexity out of the social world, reducing it to "simple" reactions

practitioners now'. Paulo Freire Centennial: 7 Talks in Preparation for the Next 100 Years, London, 9-23 March 2021, https://doi.org/10.17028/rd.lboro.14397899.v1.
4   Deane, *'Paulo Freire and Empathy and its implications for media and communication practitioners now.'*
5   Idem.
6   Idem.
7   Alejandro Barranquero, *Paulo Freire y Los Estudios de Comunicación para el Cambio Social,* trans. Fania Sánchez de la Vega, España: Universidad de Málaga, 2006.
8   Deane, *'Paulo Freire and Empathy and its implications for media and communication practitioners now.'*

of acceptance or rejection without context and reinforcing differences, widening social divisions and dichotomizing the humane world.

As a media and communication practitioner myself and a true believer in technopolitics, it's frustrating to see how many collectives, non-profits, non-governmental organizations, foundations and civil associations haven't had any alternative in the past years but to fall into the trap of digital marketing. It no longer matters what issue we're fighting for, how much a priority or how urgent our actions may be, the level of advocacy we should reach, how radical or anti-system our actions must be to achieve change. It seems nICTs (the programmers and owners) have the last word on how to use these platforms depending on what's allowed. Otherwise, we'd face an inexplicable algorithm with the power to surveille, hide and ban us. Apparently, communicating now is about excelling in how to "sell your cause" instead of giving relevant information for people's awareness.

At the risk of being wrong, I imagine if Freire were alive in this globally marketed human society, he would invite us to re-think communication as a critical pedagogical tool. This brings me to the experience that Claudia Magallanes shared about indigenous communicators and facilitators in a rural community in Mexico: community communication and popular communication are schools of life that generate alternative models of education. This model allows us to re-educate ourselves with a critical sense of the symbolic and community elements that are substantive for life, showing more dignified views of what we are and escaping from the colonizing language. This re-education also means strengthening ourselves politically, having greater elements of analysis of the realities we experience.[9]

Re-thinking the communication practice and the role of the media requires raising the political and militant dimensions of this field. And for this to happen, schools of communication with their professors at the forefront have an important task: to regain the emancipatory function of the true word by combining reflection and action.[10] The study and teaching in the field of Media and Communication has a lot to learn and apply from the theoretical-methodological proposal of Paulo Freire. It requires critical and disruptive educators who can imagine alternatives, sensitive to human complexity, politically active, and daring enough to defy hegemonic culture.

So too, media and communication practitioners have several challenges to address. Starting by un-fetishizing the media, this means identifying the limits of virtuality, the fleeting of the internet, and the simulation of social media. It is not about cancelling the digital media, but about giving them their rightful place. In other words, re-link the digital world with the analogue world. The post-pandemic message could be *let's get over the like+comment+share+save* and let's re-exist, propose, and balance the physical space with the virtual space.

9   Claudia Magallanes Blanco, '*A Dialogue on Communication from an Indigenous Perspective in Mexico*', Paulo Freire Centennial: 7 Talks in Preparation for the Next 100 Years, London, 9-23 March 2021, https://doi.org/10.17028/rd.lboro.14397941.v1.
10   Idem.

All of the above must be done with a critical hope in the Freirean perspective, that 'teaches us that there is no mobilization without prior awareness. It is necessary for people to be aware of their historical role, aware of the situation in order to mobilize'.[11] The historical perspective helps to understand that change is a pedagogical process, and like any process it takes time, it's cyclical and it may never end: socio-political awareness and collective action happen slowly. This, in a time of history where culture privileges the immediate, is disruptive itself.

To keep the process current and continuous, it is important to share the hope that other forms can be possible and that many are already real. The world, more than ever, needs pathological optimists[12] like Magallanes, Deane, Frei Betto and Paulo Freire; people capable of infusing critical hope on how communication not only presents reality but builds it.

11   Carlos Alberto Libanio Christo, 'Homage to Paulo Freire on his centenary', Paulo Freire Centennial: 7 Talks in Preparation for the Next 100 Years, London, 9-23 March 2021, https://doi.org/10.17028/rd.lboro.14398010.v1.
12   Magallanes-Blanco, A Dialogue on Communication from an Indigenous Perspective in Mexico.

LOVE AS PRAXIS: REFLECTIONS FROM THEATRE OF THE OPPRESSED MOVEMENT IN EASTERN INDIA

JHARNA BRAHMA

According to Paulo Freire, *dehumanization* is a process whereby we treat other humans as less than ourselves. When we dehumanize others, at the same time we also become less human. The dehumanized state is the *oppression,* according to Freire. Linje Manyozo, an African Communication Scholar, says that being an oppressor is a position, not an identity[1] . We may not be dehumanizing any one directly in our everyday life willingly, but in a world where there are deep and contrasting inequalities, we are very much a part of the dehumanizing system. We therefore are living as less human every day, so long as we cannot fix those inequalities.

We often do pose ourselves in solidarity with the oppressed groups and marginalized issues. However, sympathy, solidarity, and good intentions are not enough, says Paulo Freire. He asserts that liberation does not come as a gift to the oppressed, but they must fight for it.[2] It is the oppressed who must lead their own liberation. This struggle is a non-violent one and does not imitate the actions of the oppressor; this fight has the potential to free both the oppressors and the oppressed from the oppressive system.

In contrast to the definition of dehumanization, to be human would mean to treat others as ourselves, in other words, to *love* others as ourselves. Therefore, all the efforts that go into bringing fellow humans to equal and dignified positions are in this pursuit of *being more human*.[3]

Love as a revolutionary force

It was a historic moment when communication scholars across the world gathered (online) on Paulo Freire's centennial, inspired by his philosophy and writings, to refocus on some of his fundamental ideas, which are directly related to this concept of *'being human'*. In the series of the centennial talks what captivated me most is the concept of *'Love'*. It is because of its holistic nature, arching over other human virtues. Karin Wilkins, who was one of the speakers, put it so well[4] that *Love* is foundational to all other virtues: "There is no *empathy* without *Love*. *Humility* comes from *Love*. We engage in *dialogue* through *Love*. And it is because of *Love* that we have hope".

---

1   Linje Manyozo, *Communicating development with communities*, Abingdon, Oxon; New York, NY: Routledge, 2017.
2   Paulo Freire, *Pedagogy of the oppressed*, New York, NY: Herder and Herder, 1970.
3   Freire, *Pedagogy of the oppressed*.
4   https://www.paulofreirecentennial.org/videos/.

Paulo Freire's critical pedagogy is fundamentally based on *Love*, which is not a mere feeling, but involves action in liberating and uplifting other humans. Freire's *Pedagogy of the Oppressed* was inspired by Gustavo Gutierrez's Liberation Theology. In one of his latest lectures,[5] Gutierrez interpreted '*Love as action*' from the Bible. He quoted from the book of Matthew 22:37-39, where Jesus says that the greatest of all commandments is to *love God and to love your neighbor as yourself*. That sums up all of the commandments. Gutierrez says spirituality is a practice, which would mean that loving another human as yourself is spirituality.

Love is the force that moves us to do 'good works,' but genuine *Love* does not lead to what Freire calls '*false generosity*'[6] which is hegemonic and subjugates others. Wilkins also talked about *Love* as respect for others, distinct from its present-day commodification. According to the Bible, the highest form of Love is *Agape*,[7] the 'unselfish Love'. Feelings can change, but Agape is a commitment, a decision to love. So, *Love* is a spiritual practice and at the same time, a political force, according to Antonia Darder's[8] interpretation of Freire's work: 'the political significance of *Love* in the evolution of consciousness'. *Love* is also being studied as a force for social justice. Cornel West says, 'justice is what love looks like in public'.[9]

Love, therefore, is an emancipatory praxis and encompasses other human virtues such as compassion, empathy, humility, and hope. It can be expressed or translated into action through democratic engagements like listening, dialogue, awakening of critical consciousness, etc.

The following example from my own ongoing research shows how *Love* can be practiced in a social change initiative.

Jana Sanskriti's Theatre of the Oppressed movement: A Journey unfolding Love

Jana Sanskriti (JS), a Theatre of the Oppressed (TO) group operating in rural Bengal in the eastern part of India, started their journey in the early 1980s. Today they have grown and spread wide in the state of West Bengal and beyond India, and are known to be the biggest TO movement in the world.[10] JS practices Forum Theatre (FT), one of the variants of TO invented by Augusto Boal, the famous Brazilian theatre director, theorist, and activist. JS has had quite a reflexive and organic journey. The group transitioned from practicing propagandist style of dramaturgy to the current radically democratic and participatory form of theatre (FT) in the early 1990s. In their enduring journey, through my close observation, I have found that in every turn that they took with their learnings and experiences, those elemental forces of

---

5   https://www.youtube.com/watch?v=8utDwPwnzJs.
6   Freire, *Pedagogy of the oppressed*.
7   https://www.youtube.com/watch?v=slyevQ1LW7A.
8   https://www.youtube.com/watch?v=0gnvWHcf8N8.
9   https://www.coursera.org/learn/love-social-justice.
10   Julian Boal, 'It's when theatre is over that our work begins: The example of Jana Sanskriti', in D. Da Costa (eds), *Scripting power: Jana Sanskriti on and offstage,* Kolkata: CAMP, 2010, pp. 145–152.

Love, discussed above, were hidden like a treasure, determining their shifts and triggering their moves from one stage to another. These forces (like solidarity, empathy, humility, and hope) stand out quite starkly, and played a crucial role in humanizing the people who initiated this FT movement as well as the people in the community who came forward to participate in the movement.

Intellectual progress is the key to constructing human society, and theatre helps in creating an intellectual space, where actors and spectators can engage in dialogue, learn and evolve together, says Sanjoy Ganguly, the artistic director of JS.[11] The journey of JS began with a small group of disenchanted, young left-leaning political workers. One of them was Sanjoy Ganguly who, while narrating his experiences of being in the mainstream politics, said he came out of the party not being able to withstand the 'monologue', political religiosity and the bourgeois attitudes dominating the party and the regime. "I felt oppressed", he said.[12] After parting ways with the party, along with a couple of others who were then working with a local NGO, he started visiting slums near Calcutta (now Kolkata) city to connect with people at the margins. Their engagement with the people in the slums, who migrated in search of a livelihood, took them to the villages from where the slum dwellers came to the city. They went to the villages to understand the root causes of the migration.

Sanjoy Ganguly does not shy away from identifying himself as a political activist even today. He explicitly mentions that JS was born out of a political need, and he went to villages as an activist wanting to work outside party politics. Theatre eventually became a means of their political action.[13] He now refers to 'theatre as a politics',[14] unlike *political theatre* where theatre is just an extension of the party's propaganda. So, what really took him to the awful living conditions in the villages (as described by him) then,[15] leaving the comfort of city life and other possible political careers? Perhaps *Solidarity*, both as a concerned human being and arising from the political responsibility that came from the political ideology to which he held. All of that mixed in with his own political ambition, educated middle class family and cultural background, and the larger political climate prevailing in West Bengal and in India in general at that point of time.

"I got *courage* when I came in contact with JS", says Sikha, from South 24 Parganas district of West Bengal, who led the anti-liquor movement in her locality against the powerful nexus of the illicit liquor business. She wasn't directly affected by the menaces of the liquor business but she fought the good fight for the sake of other women and children of her locality. Likewise, JS grew and expanded, driven and mobilized by such intangible forces as solidarity, love and compassion that generally motivate humans to do good for others.

---

11   Sanjoy Ganguly, personal interview, 2019.
12   Ganguly, personal interview.
13   Sanjoy Ganguly, *Jana Sanskriti: Forum Theatre and Democracy in India*, Hoboken: Taylor & Francis, 2010.
14   Ganguly, *Jana Sanskriti*, p-16.
15   Ganguly, *Jana Sanskriti*, p-8.

Theatre embellished with elements of Love

FT is a theatre technique where the oppressed make and perform a play from their own lived experiences. Immediately after the performance, the Joker/facilitator opens up a forum for dialogue and a debate takes place. In that way, real dialogue is ignited through theatre performance. Based fundamentally on the principles of Freire's critical pedagogy, FT has the potential to affect and change the social reality in a way that is more humane and congenial for the oppressed to live. In the entire Forum theatre process, *Love* or its elemental forces can be seen playing a key role at every step: demolishing the inherent inhumane forces present *within* (personal) and *outside* (structural) that hinder humans (both oppressed and the oppressor) from becoming *fully human* and achieving emancipation from the dehumanized state. That is why Ganguly says FT is a rehearsal for *Total revolution*,[16] on the lines of Boal's *rehearsal for revolution*[17], meaning FT can bring about internal transformation that can eventually transform the external reality.

CRITICAL CONSCIOUSNESS

When a piece of oppressive reality is played out before an audience, comprised of both the oppressed (like the actors themselves) and the oppressors, it triggers *conscientization*[18] in both the oppressed and the oppressor. The play inspires the general public to reflect on what has been happening in their community, to individuals or groups whose lives are portrayed in the play. It hits the oppressors present as they see their actions being replayed, while it connects intimately with the oppressed among the audience.

EMPATHY

While FT creates a space for the oppressed to express their agony, their preferences, their arguments, dissensions and resolutions, the images presented also serve to generate empathy among the audience. This then helps in mobilizing people to participate in thinking about the issue and solutions for the same. Thus, it creates a space and opportunity for the oppressed to organize a real dialogue with the oppressor, the other oppressed ones, the general public and local authorities to discuss the matter and find some solution or alternative measures.

PERSONAL LIBERATION AND HOPE

Though the FT expects responses and solutions, it first aims to and has the potential to liberate the oppressed. FT is an oppressed-centered practice. It does not wait for oppressors

---

16   R. Klement, Interview with Sima and Sanjoy Ganguly, November 2013, in S. Ganguly (eds) From Boal to Jana Sanskriti, New York: Routledge, 2017, pp. 85–90.
17   {#_30j0zll .anchor} Augusto Boal, *Theater of the oppressed,* New York: Urizen Books, 1979.
18   Freire, *Pedagogy of the oppressed.*

to change; it changes the oppressed first. It liberates them from the yoke of oppression first cognitively; external manifestations sometimes occur much later. The change begins the moment they decide to resist the oppression they have been under for so long. Informants during my fieldwork have narrated their stories of personal liberation, which happened either while watching the play or while rehearsing. They described how they went back home as changed persons and how they found other ways of responding to the oppression they were experiencing every day at home. During rehearsals, while critically reflecting upon their own situation, they unwind themselves and get relief as they can share their suffering with others. They become empowered, as they begin to see and understand the root causes of the oppression to which they have been subjected, and realize that being under oppression is not their given fate. They can change their reality and they have the capacity to do it, and they will have to do it as no one else will do that for them. FT serves as a tool and a language to express and as a *'Hope'* (that reality can be changed). This *hope* is passed on to oppressed individuals with every show.

DIALOGUE, PARTICIPATION: ACTORS, SPECTATORS AND SPECTACTORS

While the actors become liberated even during the preparatory phase - scripting and rehearsing - the main purpose of public performance is to initiate a *dialogue*, generate debate and discussion. In FT, when a piece of reality is performed, it is stopped abruptly without offering any solution to the problem presented before the audience. The Joker/facilitator then invites the audience to intervene, to try to change the situation by offering their opinion and arguments. The interventionist who comes forward is called a *spectactor*.[19] He/she can come and replace the protagonist and change the scenario offering his/her opinion or solution to the problem. So, the audience members can come forward and take part in the play and ignite a real debate. The line between actors and spectators is dissolved in FT, making it dialogical. Thus, FT creates a platform for dialogue and debate in a community allowing everyone/anyone to participate in changing their social reality. These communicative spaces created through FT seem to be highly democratic, inclusive, and participatory in nature.

Theatre to Movements: changing reality

JS's FT has often been seen translated into reality. Various local movements that occurred throughout their journey testify to that. The roles of JS and FT have been to trigger or strengthen those movements, which were led by the community/oppressed people themselves. There have been movements against illegal liquor production that had led to domestic violence and other related social problems; movements against gender discrimination (child marriage, denial of education to girls, and other manifestations of patriarchal abuse) and the lack of employment for rural people. Other movements have arisen against the lack of healthcare, transport facilities and other basic necessities, as well as against the political exploitation of

19   Boal, *Theater of the oppressed.*

the poor and the marginalized.[20] These movements have been able to bring about several social changes, to which the local people, including JS actors-cum-activists, have testified in my interviews being part of those movements. The consistent process of making and performing a play, following up with the *spectactors*, various post-performance engagements in the community, formation of Human Rights Committees (now called as Responsible Citizen's Committee/RCC) by JS in the villages and continued dialogue have contributed to, and in some cases directly led, to those movements.

In all this, we can see Freire's principles of critical pedagogy consisting of the elements of *Love* running through the veins of Boal's TO in JS's practice, giving us a tangible example of how *Love* can be translated into praxis.

---

20   Jharna Brahma, Vinod Pavarala and Vasuki Belavadi, 'Driving Social Change Through Forum Theatre: A Study of Jana Sanskriti in West Bengal, India', *Asia Pacific Media Educator, 29* (2), 2019. https://doi. org/10.1177%2F1326365X19864477.

RETHINKING FREIREAN PEDAGOGY IN EDUCATION AND LEARNING IN TANZANIA

HAPPY SINGU HANSEN

During Spring 2021, I joined the seminar series *Paulo Freire Centennial* (1921-2021). Five principles of *dialogue, love, empathy, hope,* and *humility* were presented; principles and values that may appear challenged in a conflict-ridden world and may need a committed re-affirmation. This article reflects on the values and some points from presenters, while applying Freirean approaches to education and learning in Tanzania. How and to which extent are these principles relevant in Tanzania (and sub-Saharan Africa) and how can they be inspirational and useful in improving youth's learning experiences both in formal as well as informal education?

Revisiting Freire's Pedagogy

Freire is posing a humanist and liberatory pedagogy that intends to break down a rigid top-down relationship between a knowledgeable teacher and a student who 'does not know'. This hierarchy is based on 'passing down' knowledge and repetition of information which is not only ineffective as a learning model but also assumes that the student does not possess knowledge. Instead, Freire proposes co-creative ways of knowledge production leading to social changes. He argues that at any level, inside or outside the school, education must foster people's critical awareness and abilities to act and reflect on matters around them.

Freire's pedagogy focuses on learning and moves between 'doing' and 'thinking' — in relation to people's connection/relationship with their world. How people think reflects their actions and how they act reflects their thoughts. And whatever exists is based thus on human thinking and doing. Freire defines human beings as active beings who are always acting (that is also reflecting) within the world and cannot be separated from their world where their everyday realities take place. Reflections entail people's experiences and are necessary for action. Yet, because human beings are communities of being, rather than individuals[1] they cannot live alone but in relationship with each other. Actions and reflections are only meaningful when they are not dichotomized from people's interactions and relationships with each other. For that, only through communication can human life hold meaning.[2] This means that communications—interactions and relationships- are necessary conditions affecting how people learn and construct their everyday realities.

Communicative engagement influences and shapes relationships, builds personalities, facilitates (further) learning and the acquisition of knowledge and skills. Through communication - listening and speaking/telling, questioning - people can extend their horizons

---

1   Boaventura de Sousa Santos, Epistemologies of the South, London: Routledge, 2015, p.50.
2   Paolo Freire, Pedagogy of the Oppressed, London: Penguin, 1970, p. 58.

of understanding as well as develop trust and love for others. It is how we create our everyday experiences, which later come to affect our thinking and doing. Our experiences are our history and reality. Thus, Freire argued that the essence of human existence is *dialogue*. Even though authentic (or critical), *dialogue* needs *love, empathy, hope*, and *humility*. These principles are co-dependent—and are explained as follows:

To engage in *dialogue* requires us to be true to ourselves and others about our reality and struggles.[3] That's how we understand each other and establish trust which also provides a platform for growth of *love*[4] for the world and others. Love lets us relate to or identify with others, their needs, and experiences; then we enter in solidarity with them.[5] This connects us to *empathy*. Empathy, as highlighted by Manyozo, is a praxis form of conscientization, i.e., an important form of political solidarity in creating social change. This links to the point of *humility*, a principle that reminds us how it is to be a human being, that we are all equal. When engaging in dialogue as equals, we free ourselves from pride or arrogance and humble ourselves before others. We cannot encounter the world and come together as partners in social change if we lack humility.[6] Humility is a matured consciousness which requires the birth of a new *ubuntu* ('a person is a person through other people'), as Chasi noted. All this needs *intensive faith* in others. Faith is courageous, it pushes our will to act. Faith in people makes us trust their abilities and stop projecting ignorance onto others[7]

Freirean perspective sees learning as experiences which integrate culture, nature, work, and human relationships. Locating the world close to people and working from the belief that people are active actors in influencing their own lives are crucial tools for critical discovery. It allows us to think of and act in the world/reality, recognizing it as a dynamic and open space for innovation to occur. Indeed, since the purpose of education is to liberate both teacher and student, it requires the participation of both in dialogue—and in the acts of kindness. Normally, because the teacher is often regarded as oppressor, someone would say that they should be the one to (re)pay with kindness. Freire would call that a 'false solidarity.' Yet, in the Freirean perspective, the intention is not to normalise issues but to change unfavourable conditions of inequality. Students (the oppressed) must as well practice these acts of kindness. And here is where the Swahili saying comes in; *ushinde ubaya kwa wema* (in simple English translation, it means *overcome evil with good*).[8] Engaging in dialogue, love, empathy, hope, and humility, helps to avoid the situation where, instead of striving for liberation, the oppressed become oppressor (or sub-oppressor).[9]

---

3   "To speak the word is to transform the world" (Freire, 1970, p. 68) "Then you will know the truth, and the truth will set you free" (John 8:32).
4   Karin Wilkins, Paulo Freire and the principle of love in communication studies. Paulo Freire Centennial: 7 Talks in Preparation for the Next 100 Years, London, 9-23 March 2021, https://doi.org/10.17028/rd.lboro.14397959.v1.
5   Also, Freire describes love as "an act of courage, not fear, love is commitment to others" (1970, p. 70)
6   Chasi here asked: should the oppressed be humble? You are already oppressed. In the process even the oppressed should also help, be humble, to set oppressors free. To create the better not only for themselves, but also for others.
7   Freire, Pedagogy of the Oppressed.
8   Also from the bible: Romans 12:21 "Do not be overcome by evil but overcome evil with good".
9   Freire, Pedagogy of the Oppressed.

Education in Tanzania

Before colonialism, Tanzanian education was about community values. People learned through songs, dancing, listening to short stories and narratives, and participating in work such as attending cattle, cultivating the land, and cooking. Elders were responsible for teaching the younger.[10] Under German and British colonial rule (1867–1919), the indigenous cultures and education system were destroyed. Western education also created drift and frustrations between and among people. Only a few Tanzanians were selected to receive colonial education with the promise of using that education to take lower administrative and related tasks.[11]

In 1961, after Tanzania gained independence from British colonial rule, president Nyerere, introduced a fight against three enemies of development: ignorance, poverty, and diseases. In 1967, the Nyerere government adopted the *Ujamaa Policy*[12], the basis of African socialism, and a policy document named *Education for Self-Reliance* (ESR). These aimed to create a new collective agency working for/with the community and building a reliance that was local and national. People were encouraged to go back to their villages to engage in agricultural activities and create their own development paths. In addition to ESR, a *Universal Education for All* (UPE) plan was introduced in 1974 to ensure that every Tanzanian would receive primary education. This forced the establishment of infrastructure (schools) and recruitment of more teachers to make space for pupils. However, the process was established fast for a large and growing population—and furthermore for a population with a strong percentage of youth (today over half of the population is under 25). This produced a lack of trained teachers. Inexperienced teachers were brought in, and they could only reproduce or imitate older learning content or textbooks – or 'repeat information,'[13] as my father told me in a recent conversation reflecting on education in his later childhood. This is what Freire warned against - or 'taught as a finished product', in John Dewey's words.[14] Curricula did not naturally develop through interaction and adaptation. Content was merely imitated.

Although the *Education for Self-Reliance* reform tried to adapt to African ways, it was still operating under a centralized system of governance. All decisions were made from the top. In tandem with the expansion of schools and teachers, Tanzania faced an economic crisis in the

---

10   Edmond W. Siwale and Mohamed M. Sefu, 'The Development of Primary Education in Tanzania', 1977.
11   Having education and salaried jobs, they started to despise manual labor and to disrespect their parents and others who did not have the colonial education Inferiority complexes became an issue (Siwale and Sefu, 1977).
     People were aspiring to be like the white colonizers; their minds were colonised. This is what Walter Rodney calls Education for Underdevelopment.
     Rodney, Walter. How Europe Underdeveloped Africa, Cape Town: S.A. Pambazuka Press, 1972/2012, p.19.
12   See Paul Bjerk, Julius Nyerere, Ohio University Press, 2017; Goran Hyden, Beyond Ujamaa in Tanzania, London: Heinemann, 1980; Edmond W. Siwale and Mohamed M. Sefu, 'The Development of Primary Education in Tanzania'.
13   Siwale and Mohamed M. Sefu, 'The Development of Primary Education in Tanzania'.
14   John Dewey, Experience and Education, Touchstone edition, New York: Simon & Schuster, 1938/1997, p.19.

1980s, war with Uganda, and pressure from the World Bank and international organizations to take on a neoliberal approach to development. Then, in the 1990's, the country adopted the neoliberal policies that opened the doors for many private schools, including English medium schools. The focus on expanding the educational system and assuring access for every Tanzanian child remained strong. Yet, little has been done to address and achieve a certain *quality* of schooling—which also involves strong attention to methods, pedagogies, and update of curriculum.[15]

A challenge of inexperienced teachers has instead led to inexperienced 'voda fasta' teachers - providing services fast, nicknamed after the phone company, Vodacom.[16] Teachers are forced to pay themselves from an already insufficient salary for extra education[17], which halts the process of better training.[18] In addition to this systemic problem of a lack of trained teachers comes the related problem of student drop-outs, in part caused by students not finding the education relevant[19]. This mismatch contributes to the huge challenge of youth unemployment. [20] The country has not only failed in its war against the three declared enemies but gained more enemies such as inequality and corruption.[21]

Femina in Tanzania

The civil society organization (CSO) 'Femina' was established in Tanzania in 1999 primarily as a health platform for 13-30 year old Tanzanians, responding to HIV/AIDS challenges (but also including sexual health and rights in decision making) through educational entertainment.[22] Within years it achieved a nationwide scope, reaching up to a third of the country's youth

15   In 1999 Tanzania adopted the program known as The Tanzania Development Vision 2025.
     Arun R. Joshi, and Isis Gaddis, eds, Preparing the next generation in Tanzania: Challenges and opportunities in education, The World Bank: 2015; Christine Valente, 'Primary Education Expansion and Quality of Schooling: Evidence from Tanzania', 2015.
16   Society perceived them as unqualified teachers because of the short training which made them be nicknamed as voda fasta in relation to the Vodacom mobile phone company's advertisement on how fast they can provide their services to their customers when compared to other mobile phone service providers.
     Benjamin Mbeba Meli, Relevance of In-service-Teacher Training in Tanzania: Lessons from Licensed and Normal Trained Teachers, 2020.
17   Benjamin Mbeba Meli, Relevance of In-service-Teacher Training in Tanzania: Lessons from Licensed and Normal Trained Teachers.
18   Curricula began to change, but again with a pace that made teachers disoriented. Teachers were brought in to teach subjects they are not ready to teach. The uncoordinated effort of curriculum development opted teachers to rely on the follow, repeat and memorize methods, rather than problem-solving, partly due to teachers not mastering the subjects.
19   UN (Unesco and Unicef). Tanzania Verification of the Out-of-school Children Study, March 2018.
20   Hong, Tan, Sajitha Bashir, and Nobuyuki Tanaka. Skill use, skill deficits, and firm performance in formal sector enterprises: evidence from the Tanzania enterprise skills survey, 2015, The World Bank: 2016.
21   Ansbert Ngurumo. Forty years of our fight against poverty, ignorance and diseases: Have we obtained our goal, Maendeleo Dialogue, Democracy in Tanzania, 2010.
     Edson Mwabukojo. Mapping the Development Progress in Tanzania since Independence, 2019, p. 1-88.
22   Femina Hip, annual reports, Dar es Salaam: 2017.

through a variety of media platforms involving magazines, social media, radio, television and the establishment of a youth network of what is called *Fema clubs*. 'Fema' refers to 'female-male', allowing for a more equal emphasis on involvement of both genders.

The organization has been evolving since it was established, trying to adapt and respond to youth's needs. In 2011 Femina broadened the work to economic empowerment - this through e.g., a project called *Ruka juu* (jumping up), which responded to youth participants' demands for knowledge about entrepreneurship, organization, and business. 'It is all well and good to learn about HIV/AIDS and reproductive health, but we need jobs!'.[23] Young people (as do older) in Tanzania depend to a strong extent on the informal sector economy. Jobs are often created through self and micro entrepreneurship activities. Femina realized a need[24] to integrate youth engagement and participation, as well as rights and responsibilities in a more systematic way.[25] Currently, Femina's strategic objectives are threefold: to promote sexual and reproductive health and rights, economic empowerment, and to strengthen citizen engagement.[26]

The organization aims to collaborate with existing institutions, go into the schools, and engage with teachers. Femina member youths create their own clubs together with teachers, as Fema clubs mentors. When they form a club, they register with Femina to get information and magazines, invitations to seminars and visits from Femina for interaction and guidance. The youth can get certificates at Fema clubs for completing projects which provide them with a range of life skills and then use these in their job and education searches. This forms part of the community mobilization where youth and facilitators interact through a voluntary framework. Often it works as a win-win; students get new peer learning experience, more resources, and a new learning relationship with adults. The work also offers the teacher to take on another role, as a mentor-discussant, on issues beyond the curriculum. The student chooses the mentor.

The citizen engagement dimension is nurtured through media work, such as magazines, radio, TV social media and the supporting Fema clubs in schools. These are formed and run by students (Fema clubbers) who are engaged in mobilizing support from communities, local government, and strategic partners across Tanzania. The stories they develop in their media work draw from ordinary people's experiences as sources for inspiration or ways of dealing with problems. Systems of tutorial are established through 'ask uncle' and 'ask aunt' letterboxes in the magazines. That takes on actual practices from around the country, for

---

23   Audience feedback to Femina as part of Ruka Juu.
     Ylva Ekström & Linda Helgesson Sekei. 'Citizen engagement through SMS', in Tina Askanius and Liv
     Stubbe Østergaard (eds), Reclaiming the Public Sphere, London: Palgrave, 2014., p. 184.
24   A need was realised after dealing with the last two presidential elections and the review of the
     constitution, as well as Fema Club formation and self-organising for civil society activism.
25   Femina Hip, annual reports, Dar es Salaam: 2018, p. 5.
26   My PhD research in progress engages with citizen engagement through an analysis of media materials
     and empirical data production with different generations of Femina youth, facilitators, and educators to
     address the actual experiences, reflections on, and benefits of Femina work over the years. The thesis
     thus aims for an extensive youth engagement and critical discussion around how/and to which extent
     various pedagogies, focusing on Freirean principles, have been applied in practice.

example on ways to establish toilets, environmental conservation, and so forth. The magazines, with youth produced content, are made in sparkly colors representing the youth's own aspirations, and they primarily use the national language Swahili.

As an example, I can mention a former Fema club member, Rebecca Gyumi, who then volunteered and worked at Femina and continued to establish her own organisation which fought against early marriage law. She helped push for new laws. Fema youth thereby not only get skills for the job and education market, but for creating a different society and new kinds of jobs. Fema itself becomes a cradle for formulating change. A Fema family, as they call it, wants their children to articulate and continue into a better world - through dialogue, hope, faith, and empathy - and maybe also humility.

Femina encourages new ways of formulating change and learning, drawing from a collective (including those regularly invisible), but channelled into media stories for all, which youth collaboratively collect and present. This formula, Freirean in character, can with Mulgan's words be seen as a form of *social innovation*, a praxis and body of knowledge coming into life as an evolving practice, or a form of loosely structured movement driven by the key idea that in the right circumstances people can make an impact and participate in shaping their world. [27]

We may call Femina's work a key example of applications of *communication* (or *education*) *for social change*, relying on civic engagement, yet it also has an organizational structure that, to a strong extent, relies on continuous foreign funding from notably Scandinavian aid programmes and embassies.

Conclusion

Issues such as active citizenship (civic engagement), leadership, agency, voice and equality, in part drawing from Freire's thinking and others such as John Dewey, have influenced the ways that educational institutions, organizations, and companies approach education—particularly in the Western world, notably Scandinavia.

In the case of Tanzania, Nyerere's Ujama policy and ESR had a decolonization perspective, which may have failed even without the pressure from Western countries, or other challenges, but importantly, because it lacked a *participatory approach*. Although there were some attempts at participation, the education system was strongly centralized. This hierarchical teacher-student relationship continues to influence the education structure today even after some reforms.

From a Freirean perspective, critical education is emphasized because it is an attempt to fill people with critical awareness—which is important to change the oppressive power structures and work towards equality and social justice. 'Social change' in this case, are the words for

---

27   See Alex Nicholls, Julie Simon and Madeleine Gabriel, New frontiers in social innovation research, Springer Nature, 2015, p xi.

(social) *innovation* where we either create something totally new (that has never existed) or revitalise old values and knowledge to create the new. However, in any meaningful social change, people's participation and inclusion in genuine dialogue and the decision-making process are necessary—and must be the focus of education for social change.

The CSO Femina tries to reintroduce a foundational participatory approach, filling the puzzle, highlighting and connecting pieces from the communities. They aim to listen to and have faith in youth – and use old and modern forms of communication that reflect not only on new ideas, but also on historic traditions and values of contemporary relevance.

REFLECTING PAULO FREIRE ON COMMUNICATION FOR SOCIAL CHANGE IN THE DIGITAL AGE

MICHAEL DOKYUM KIM

I first came across Paulo Freire's seminal work *Pedagogy of the Oppressed* six years ago when I started my master's program in Media, Communication and Development at the London School of Economics and Political Science.[1] As I undoubtedly presume many others would have (or will) experienced the same, the book became one of the most influential pieces that reshaped my visions and ideas about approaching communication and social change. This eventually led me to pursue an academic career, currently in a doctoral program studying 'communication for social change' with a slant of critical perspective following Freire's lessons. Embarrassing as it may sound in hindsight, my first reaction to Freire's piece may be easily imaginable confessing that I started the master's program hoping to become an 'expert' in handling communication for social change (C4SC) as if communication was a one-size-fits-all technique or skill one could simply master and apply in the various contexts of development and change.

Six years have passed since my first encounter with the book. Newly introduced communication technologies in the past six years are countless. This is an age where a communication technology that was science-fictional yesterday could become a reality tomorrow. The exponential rate of technological advancement in communication will indeed introduce a variety of new functions to be utilized for social change. However, challenges to C4SC also loom large in the age of technological advancement. In this brief reflection, I bring Freire's lessons on communication and social change and reflect on the challenges to C4SC in the digital age. This reflection is inspired by the contributors of the *Paulo Freire Centennial Conference,* who have motivated me to re-engrave the invaluable lessons of Paulo Freire.[2] I begin by outlining the key takeaways of Freire's visions of communication and social change, namely his notions of dialogue and *critical consciousness*, which are set against the dominant ideas of communication and social change in the digital age, the spirit of techno-centrism, and the resultant *technocentric consciousness*.

Freire's principles of 'communication' and 'social change' are manifest through his notions of *dialogue* and *critical consciousness* (*conscientização*). Dialogue, which is profoundly inscribed into his pedagogy, is different from a linear conversation where messages simply transfer back and forth between individuals momentarily. Instead, dialogue refers to a circular and permanent communication process of achieving a shared understanding whereby individuals are required to and able to engage in a reflective participation. It is a reflective process in a sense that one recognizes the value of oneself equally as others (humility), one is able to be in others' shoes to see injustices and differences (empathy), one can embrace those differences (love), and strive

---

1   Paulo Freire, Pedagogy of the Oppressed, London: Penguin Books, 1996.
2   Paulo Freire Centennial: 7 Talks in Preparation for the Next 100 Years, Conference by The Institute for Media and Creative Industries at Loughborough University London, 9-24 March, 2021, https://www. paulofreirecentennial.org/principal-in/.

towards justice and coexistence (hope).[3] Therefore, unlike any one-way communication process such as persuasion, the dialogic process recognizes the value of self-reflection and individual agency of those participating in the circular communication, making sure everyone have a say. As Freire would argue, dialogue goes hand in hand with the notion of *critical consciousness*.

Critical consciousness is differentiated from the more basic meaning of consciousness. Whereas consciousness simply refers to an 'awareness of oneself,' critical consciousness pushes beyond self-awareness and emphasizes an 'inquiry into oneself.' If having a consciousness helps us realize 'who we are,' critical consciousness prepares us to ask ourselves *why* we are 'who we are' and *what* does it mean to be 'who we are' in a particular social, cultural, economic, and political context. In this sense, critical consciousness refers to both an in-depth situational self-awareness and an ability to throw questions at and act against our possible surroundings of oppressive and unjust context.[4] Hence, dialogue and critical consciousness complement each other. By stressing individual agency and mutual understanding, dialogue offers a ground for critical consciousness to sprout, and critical consciousness permanently activates dialogue. Therefore, the dialogic process for social change cannot be arranged from above by an external agent in a top-down manner. For Freire, the oppressed are not liberated by the external agents, but by the internal agents themselves who are able to realize their positions of oppression, which then become stepping-stones for change.

Against the dominant ideas of social change which maintained top-down C4SC interventions, Freire's visions of dialogue and critical consciousness paved the way for alternative understandings of C4SC in the 1970s and onward, expressed in various notions such as "participatory," "local" and "another" communication for social change. These alternative approaches refuted the universal idea of modernization as the only path to social change and emphasized the human elements over material elements in the process of social change manifested through notions of agency and culture. However, regardless of the decades of critical lessons we have been reminded of since Freire, these alternatives seem to remain in the level of 'alternatives' rather than rising to the level of 'mainstream', especially in the digital age. The problem may not be ascribed to the turn of the new digital era marked by Industrial Revolution 4.0, yet as research shows, the digitization of communication technologies is undoubtedly bringing the previous model of social change back to the fore with an accelerated pace.[5] As much as technological advancement and digitization are expected to extend the functions

3   Ana C. Suzina and Thomas Tufte, 'Freire's Vision of Development and Social Change: Past Experiences, Present Challenges and Perspectives for the Future', *The International Communication Gazette* 82.5 (2020): 411-424.

4   Gayatri C. Spivak, 'Can the Subaltern Speak?', in Cary Nelson and Lawrence Grossberg (eds) *Marxism and the Interpretation of Culture*, Basingstoke: Macmillan, 1988, p. 271.

5   Robin Mansell, 'Power and Interests in Information and Communication and Development: Exogenous and Endogenous Discourses in Contention', *Journal of International Development* 26 (2014): 109-127; Christine L. Ogan, Manaf Bashir, Lindita Camaj, Yunjuan Luo, Brian Gaddie, Rosemary Pennington, Sonia Rana and Mohammed Salih, 'Development Communication: The State of Research in an Era of ICTs and Globalization', *The International Communication Gazette* 71.8 (2009): 655-670; Michael D. Kim and Kyung Sun Lee, 'Ten years of ICT4D research in development communication: From 2009 to 2019', International Association for Media and Communication Research Annual Conference, Tampere, 12-17 July 2020, https://iamcr.org/tampere2020/papers.

of society, it will also hasten losing sight of Freire's critical lessons of 'communication' and 'social change' under the wave of *techno-centrism*, which is a value system that is centered on technology and its ability to control the social reality and the environment.

Techno-centrism focuses on the existence and ability of technology itself rather than on how technology is controlled and contextualized by the people. The challenges to C4SC in the digital age arise from this tendency to imbue technology's existence a meaning 'on its own,' while downplaying the human elements that in fact 'give meanings' to the existence of technology. Under techno-centrism, as long as smartphones can offer a particular function, then who enables that function, who is excluded from that function, and what people make of that function become secondary concerns. Likewise, the 'digital' in the 'digital age' becomes a separate reality existing on its own outside the realm of human agency. This way, it is something over which one cannot have control or even avoid. Digitization, then becomes a social trend in which individuals have no choice but to hop on and adapt to it.

In this sense, notions such as 'network', 'community', and 'participation' are more *pre-given* by the affordances of technology and what technology can do, rather than *achieved* through human struggle and action. Eventually, digital communication technologies are regarded as the agents of change on their own, wherein technological development is seen as equivalent to social progress. 'Human agency' is, therefore, abstracted and replaced by the 'technological agency.' Communication technologies supplement conversations but not dialogue, and datafication and algorithms supplement consciousness that is technocentric but not critical. The notions of communication and social change in the digital age are likely to be oblivious to the Freirean lessons of dialogue and critical consciousness.

A concern is raised against this trend of what I call *technocentric consciousness* in the sphere of C4SC as it is likely to bring back the functionalist, linear, and non-participatory paradigm of communication and change. Perhaps this trend has been hastened by the outbreak of COVID-19 pandemic, which has brought us into the 'new normal' life, within which our reliance on digital technology has been extended. A survey conducted by McKinsey & Company, a US-based management consulting firm, reveals that responses to COVID-19 have accelerated the adoption of digitization in businesses by several years.[6]

However, we must ask whether this conception of 'normal' applies equally across individuals in their intersectionality. For the digitally privileged, the 'new normal' may simply be just another version of 'normal,' being able to attend online classes, able to work at home with portable devices, and able to maintain their living without having to expose themselves to the virus. But for many, this new version of 'normal' is an ever more compounded version of struggle; a struggle that should never be called 'normal.' And it is likely that their struggles will not be recognized unless they adapt to the new reality driven by digitization, that will accelerate in time. Even if they are recognized, the solutions to these struggles are likely to be suggested based on

---

6   McKinsey & Company, https://www.mckinsey.com/business-functions/strategy-and-corporate-finance/
     our-insights/how-covid-19-has-pushed-companies-over-the-technology-tipping-point-and-transformed-
     business-forever.

technocentric approaches with the use of big data and algorithms, leaving no room for critical consciousness of the oppressed.

A good example in which these problems are visible is in the sphere of digital humanitarianism. Social media and other big data sources are increasingly changing the ways crises and emergencies are addressed by allowing timely and extensive data (both citizen-generated and real-time data) to monitor and assess the situation. However, often the 'local data' collected are not only unrepresentative of the local knowledge but also undergo a number of mutations as they are transferred between the data collectors, data analysts, and the decision-makers.[7] Even so, the decisions are often based on the methods privileged by technocentric consciousness of mathematics and correlations that are deemed 'scientific' and 'technological,' rather than on methods that value qualitative understanding, communal and situated knowledges, and their contextual connections among people.[8]

In the preface of the *Pedagogy of the Oppressed*, Freire makes a distinction between sectarianism and radicalization. To rephrase and reinterpret his distinction for our purpose, sectarianism, on the one hand, is nourished by uncritical fervor for technology and leads to disintegrated visions of change. Radicalization, on the other, is nourished by critical spirit against this fervor and leads to creative and liberating visions of change.[9] Technocentric consciousness driven by datafication and algorithms is sectarian in nature. Fanatic to the pre-existing reality of the 'digital world' external to the human agency, algorithms are designed to categorize subjects within this reality under the labels of 'mathematic' and 'scientific' approaches and reproduce the categorized subjects accordingly. Datafied human agency exists to strengthen the power of algorithms, only to return to the social, to be categorized in terms of race, gender, class, nationality, credit score and the like. Algorithms, then mathematically decide what is normal and abnormal, further disintegrating the oppressed rather than liberating them.

In the digital age, the oppressed (not just those socio-economically marginalized, but all of us whose critical consciousness is threatened by technocentric consciousness) eventually find a new oppressor, which is not only the big data companies but also the oppressed themselves who unwittingly contribute to this uncritical fervor. It is not smartphones that make us smarter; instead, it is we who make smartphones smarter. Consequently, digitization and algorithms resuscitate the top-down mechanism. Coupled with the commodification of digital data in which human collected data is treated as products, such a trend will ever more limit the opportunities for critical consciousness, and therefore, dialogue.

As a doctoral student as well as a would-be academic, these regimes of the digital age present both practical opportunities and challenges to the research and education of C4SC.

7   Femke Mulder, Julie Ferguson, Peter Groenewegen, Kees Boersma and Jeroen Wolbers, 'Questioning Big Data: Crowdsourcing Crisis Data Towards an Inclusive Humanitarian Response', *Big Data & Society* 3.2 (December, 2016): 1-13.
8   Ryan Burns, 'Rethinking big data in digital humanitarianism: practices, epistemologies, and social relations', *GeoJournal* 80 (October, 2014): 477-490.
9   Paulo Freire, Pedagogy of the Oppressed, London: Penguin Books, 1996, p. 19.

Opportunity-wise, constant innovations of various communication technologies will offer endless topics of inquiries in need of exploration and empirical examination. In other words, research topics will never run out! However, challenges are preeminent as these inquiries will more likely be answered from the functionalist rather than critical perspectives. As discussed above, the technocentric regime will only expand and is likely to sideline the need for critical education further. Even if it is not sidelined, the speed of innovation in communication technology will not wait for the critical understanding of that same technology to catch up. In fact, techno-centrism has already infiltrated into their youth education curriculums in countries such as Singapore, South Korea, United States, and United Kingdom. In 2019, South Korea, for example, has implemented a mandatory 17 hours of 'Coding' education for primary schools, through which young pupils learn how to develop programs, make decisions, and solve problems with them. Future academics and practitioners alike will have to overcome this already-imbalanced supply and demand of critical pedagogy and linear pedagogy in order to preserve Freire's lessons in C4SC.

Allow me to conclude by reminding us of the essence of Freire's lessons in C4SC. Social change happens not simply by people coming together to gain knowledge of their social reality. Therefore, communication in social change must not be understood simply as an information dissemination process or even as an information utilization process. Knowledge must entail critical reflection upon their reality and action upon their environment. Therefore, communication in social change must be understood as a negotiation process channeling critical reflection and action'. Also, social change cannot be achieved through any abstract entity exogenous to human agency however advanced and innovative a technology may be, but through permanent process of this reflection and action grounded in human agency. Thus, Freire reminds us to appreciate the process of change over the result of change. Without the process that values the voices and the agency of the oppressed, the result will only replicate the injustices, which may be digitally driven yet mirror the existing injustices on the ground.

COMMUNICATING FOR OR WITH THE OTHER? REFLECTIONS ON FREIRE'S DIALOGUE AND EMPATHY IN THE SOUTH AFRICAN COVID-19 COMMUNICATION RESPONSE

NOMPUMELELO GUMEDE

Introduction

> There are many challenges that we've faced; like I had to make sure that I have enough masks because if people arrive and they are not wearing masks I have to provide them with one. I also have to have a sanitizer to keep us safe. In order to help someone, I have to pray for them, and you can't not place your hands on them. You perform the cutting rituals, you bath people, but you are also afraid that you may get infected, but you can't avoid it because you have to help a person so that they get well. It's been very difficult. Traditional Healer, Umlazi Township, South Africa[1]

This is a statement from one of the participants in my current PhD study exploring a culture-centered approach to COVID-19 communication in township, rural and informal settlement areas in KwaZulu-Natal, South Africa.

In reflecting on the concepts of dialogue and empathy as espoused by Paulo Freire, I connect these reflections to my experience as a researcher and a practitioner in health communication. While this traditional healer's words relate to her experiences with COVID-19 prevention in a township setting in South Africa, her voice is a representation of an all-too-familiar dilemma in health communication practice where communication is often misconstrued to mean 'simply sending messages' to a naïve public and expecting 'change to follow'.[2]

While uniform broadcast messages disseminated by government have enabled a degree of knowledge acquisition to the traditional healer, the reality of her healing practice prevents her from being able to fully protect herself from the risk of COVID-19. Her voice remains at the margins, silenced by the hegemonic communication approach that has been adopted in communicating COVID-19 preventive messages, despite lessons having been learnt with previous epidemics of Ebola and HIV and AIDS about the ineffectiveness of such an approach.

---

1   Research participant. 'Umlazi WhatsApp Community Dialogue'. Durban, South Africa, 2021.
2   Wendy Quarry and Ricardo Ramirez, 'Communication for Development: setting the scene.' in Wendy Quarry and Ricardo Ramirez, *Communication for another development: listening before telling*, London: Zed Books, pp. 5-22.

The principles of dialogue and empathy are two of five principles isolated by Suzina and Tufte[3] and which reverberate throughout the works of Paulo Freire over time. These principles (dialogue, love, empathy, hope and humility) continue to influence research and practice in the field of health communication amongst researchers and practitioners who align themselves with Freire's 'ontological call' that is rooted in Marxist philosophy. As I reflect on Freire's principles of dialogue and empathy, I highlight the challenges in applying them in health communication research and practice, and what the implications of these are for my own research.

The South African COVID-19 communication response

The South African COVID-19 communication strategy is coordinated through the government's central communication agency, the Government Communication and Information Services (GCIS). The strategy involves the dissemination of information through paid-for advertisements in electronic and print broadcasting, including community media, as well as media engagement and the use of government digital media platforms, including social media channels.

While the country's response to containing the spread of COVID-19 has been applauded by some, calls have also been made for the engagement and mobilization of communities, as the response to HIV/AIDS showed that when people are meaningfully engaged, they are able to contribute to meaningful solutions and innovations.[4] The main criticism for this one-way, top-down communication approach is its propensity for stifling public participation and failing to integrate local knowledge and contexts.

In the fight against HIV and AIDS in South Africa and elsewhere, community mobilization, social capital development, dialogue, and empowerment led to sustainable local responses to community health problems.[5] In responding to the Ebola outbreaks of 2012 and 2015 in West African countries, the lack of authentic dialogue with communities was associated with increased reluctance and resistance by local communities to adopt the recommended Ebola prevention measures.[6]

---

3   Ana Cristina Suzina and Thomas Tufte, 'Freire's vision of development and social change: Past experiences, present challenges and perspectives for the future', *International Communication Gazette*. 2020;82(5): 411-424. doi:10.1177/1748048520943692.
4   United Nations South Africa, *United Nations Commends South Africa Response to the COVID-19 pandemic*, http://www.un.org.za/press-release-united-nations-commends-south-africas-response-to-the-covid-19-pandemic/, 4 June 2020.
5   Catherine Campbell and Flora Cornish, 'Towards a "fourth generation" of approaches to HIV/AIDS management: creating contexts for effective community mobilization', *AIDS care*, No. sup2 (2010): 1569-1579.
6   Sylla Thiam, Alexandre Delamou, Soriba Camara, Jane Carter, Eugene Kaman Lama, Bara Ndiaye, Josephat Nyagero, John Nduba and Mor Ngom, 'Challenges in controlling the Ebola outbreak in two prefectures in Guinea: why did communities continue to resist?' *The Pan African Medical Journal*, (2015): 22(Suppl 1).

The South African COVID-19 communication response then provides us with a backdrop against which we can discuss the challenges and complexities of integrating the principles of dialogue and empathy in health communication, and in communication for social change in general.

Dialogue

COVID-19 communication practice in the South African context remains monologic with persuasion messages sent out to communities in the hope that community members will change what may be perceived as risky behaviors or adopt new behaviors. This is what Hook, Franks and Bauer have termed 'anti-dialogue', an approach to health communication that has historically placed 'health professionals' in the position of the 'experts' who possess the most accurate knowledge about health, while at the same time placing the 'uneducated' public at the opposite end of the education spectrum.[7]

Blanco's[8] conceptualization of Freire's principle of dialogue is that of genuine two-way communication where there is mutual recognition. In the case of the traditional healer referred to earlier in this article, authentic dialogue would not only be about message dissemination, but also about listening with the aim of gaining an understanding of the peculiarities of her practice and then to work with her to formulate workable strategies that can enable her to fulfill her healing responsibility to the community, while also protecting herself from COVID-19.

In my PhD study, I engage in a process of virtual community dialogues through the medium of WhatsApp chat groups. These community dialogues with community members afford me the opportunity to engage in what Blanco terms 'critical dialogue' that is anchored in peoples' contexts[9]. This dialogic engagement with communities in my research provides a window into communities' experiences as they grapple with challenges imposed upon them by COVID-19 restrictions, while also trying to keep themselves safe from infection.

Empathy

In his reflection on Paulo Freire's concept of empathy, Manyozo states that 'empathy... allows us to enter into worlds we are not familiar with.'[10] In reflecting on the principle of empathy, I consider Suzina and Tufte's assertion that empathy is not about charity or generosity, but rather 'a form of recognizing different points of departure that make it harder for some to reach their

7   Derek Hook, Bradley Franks and Martin Bauer (Eds), *The social psychology of communication*, New York: Palgrave McMillan, 2011.
8   Claudia Magallanes-Blanco, *A Dialogue from an Indigenous Perspective in Mexico*. Loughborough University. Media, 2021. https://doi.org/10.17028/rd.lboro.14397941.v1
9   Claudia Magallanes Blanco, *A Dialogue from an Indigenous Perspective in Mexico*.
10   Linje Manyozo, *On Empathy for the Other*. Loughborough University. Media, 2021. https://doi.org/10.17028/rd.lboro.14397968.v1

goals.'[11] The field of health communication and behavior change is littered with Euro-Western-centric forms of theorizing that prioritize the individual over the collective. As a result, the collectivist nature of most African societies is ignored, and solutions to health challenges are almost always conceptualized from this individual focus. The concept of empathy affords us the opportunity to enter others' worlds through a dialogic process that exposes the systemic nature of oppression and opens up space for it to be challenged and changed. Lubombo and Dyll[12] have proposed an approach based on the principles of respect, humanity and interconnectedness embodied in the concept of Ubuntu, as a way to operationalize empathy.

In practice, if the South African communication response to COVID-19 had been informed by the principle of empathy, the traditional health sector would have been prioritized equal to the Western-informed health sector in terms of formulating guidelines for prevention of COVID-19. As it stands currently, traditional healers in South Africa are not provided with personal protective equipment (PPE), and there are no safety guidelines that pertain to the peculiarities of their practice as a sector.

Conclusion

As I explore culture-centered health communication in my study, I grapple with and ponder the challenge articulated by Tacchi on the pervasiveness and persistence of the modernization paradigm that continues to dominate much of the practice and execution of international development projects despite 'all attempts to challenge or subvert it'.[13] In advocating for scholarship that foregrounds African ways of knowing in health communication, Airhihenbuwa argues for the need for scholarship that 'questions the question' and which problematizes the persistent application of individual-based theories of behavior change in addressing health challenges.[14]

As an African scholar and practitioner in health communication, I believe that Freire's principles of dialogue and empathy are intertwined and afford us the opportunity to challenge the silencing of voices that continue to remain at the margins. In his seminal work, *Pedagogy of the Oppressed*[15], Paulo Freire argues that it is only through communication that human life holds meaning. The principles of dialogue and empathy that I reflect upon foreground the

11   Ana Cristina Suzina and Thomas Tufte, 'Freire's vision of development and social change: Past experiences, present challenges and perspectives for the future'.
12   Musara Lubombo & Lauren Eva Dyll, 'A Dialectic Analysis of Views on Participation in HIV/AIDS Communication of Selected South African People Living with HIV/AIDS: Beyond the Greater Involvement of People Living with HIV/AIDS', *Critical Arts*, 32:2, (2018):100-118, DOI: 10.1080/02560046.2018.1434218.
13   Jo Tacchi, 'Meaningful Mobilities', in Jo Tacchi and Thomas Tufte (Eds), *Communicating for Change: Concepts to think with*, Plagrave McMillan, 2020. https://doi.org/10.1007/978-3-030-42513-5_9.
14   Collins Airhihenbuwa, '2007 SOPHE Presidential Address: On Being Comfortable With Being Uncomfortable: Centering an Africanist Vision in Our Gateway to Global Health', *Health Education & Behavior* 34, no. 1 (2007): 31–42. https://doi.org/10.1177/1090198106291377.
15   Paolo Freire, 'Pedagogy of the oppressed (revised).' *New York: Continuum* (1996).

centrality of communication as a tool for liberation and for the amplification of marginalized voces in health communication practice.

EDUCATION IS AN ACTION OF LOVE ENGAGED IN PREVENTING OTHERS FROM FEELING THE PAIN YOU FELT

ELIJERTON VERAS

My name is Elijerton Veras. I am Brazilian, married, I have a 15-year-old daughter and I have lived in Rio de Janeiro for over 27 years. I am also a professor of undergraduate courses and technical courses for low-income youth and juvenile offenders, as well as a doctoral student at the Postgraduate Program in Media and Everyday Life (PPGMC), at *Universidade Federal Fluminense* (UFF).

My history in education began with an approval for undergraduate teaching. However, as a matter of market demand, I was reassigned to technical education for the social inclusion of juvenile offenders. In addition to this offer, I also ended up getting involved in the education of young people from the periphery of the State of Rio de Janeiro.

Due to an administrative deficiency of the State, those who generally coordinate this model of education are NGOs, from the introduction of public funds and partnerships with private companies. An example of this is the *Jovem Aprendiz*,[1] a program that offers professional training to young people and benefits companies with qualified labor.

However, the context of this relationship is almost always structured in managements linked to politics/economy. That is, with regard to NGOs, relationships are based on the distribution of positions fostered by connections between political parties and supporters, with private companies and to obtain tax benefits.

Therefore, working with the education of young people from the periphery is not something simple. A condition of adaptability to the student's universe is necessary, as well as the ability to subvert the structural logic of the institutions that apply this education model. Thus, the teacher needs to strengthen the relationship with the student. S/He needs to delve into his everyday experiences; to speak their language, experience their customs, their pains, etc. In addition, one must be the agent capable of making work a structure that was made not to work.

In view of this, the project I entered had a much more commercial than social character. Thus, to generate small real transformations in the lives of excluded young people, I did what Certeau[2] called a "poaching". In other words, I transformed the classroom space of a private educational institution, a place purely dedicated to the accumulation of capital, into the

---

1   The Apprenticeship Law (Young Apprentice Program) aims to promote social and professional inclusion, offering technical-professional training to young people aged between 14 and 24 who are studying elementary or high school or who have completed high school, according to the legislation. Available at: https://www.rj.senac.br/jovem-aprendiz/.
2   Michel de Certeau, A invenção do Cotidiano, 1994.

production of its own lexicon and directed it to the exercise of social recognition/social role of each individual disposed there.

Over the course of three years, I witnessed emblematic stories of young people with no prospects for life who managed to ascend to higher education and to positions that were previously unattainable, even in their dreams. However, from mid-2018 until the present moment, a strategic abandonment of this format of training programs was started and an explicit amplification of class, race and gender prejudices, among others, was disseminated in sociotechnical networks and extended to the daily lives of these groups.

In that same vein, I saw how all these misfortunes were discursively linked to the left and to the image of Paulo Freire. I saw how traditional media and alternative media blocs orchestrated the tragedies of the economy and education. They created responsible monsters and built outlandish solutions that only favored the economic elites. In these solutions, such as the labor and social security reforms, the working class was the one that most lost rights.

Therefore, it was this perception of tragedy, the understanding of the role of the researcher/teacher in the transformation of history, the commitment to guarantee the rights of these minorities and the seminar on Paulo Freire's centenary that took me out of inertia and out of the lack of understanding of my social role. Now I'm sure I can be part of the construction of a less painful story than the one that dominates current ideas.

Recognizing this, the seminar plunged me into a state of double consciousness. It not only shaped my research, but it gave meaning to my work. It made me realize that the tragedy (political, humanitarian and social) that was approaching my country had its own didactics. And in these didactics, one of the pillars was the deconstruction of the state of "Dialogue", of "Love", of "Empathy", of "Hope" and of "Humility". That is, Paulo Freire's public image and all of his work.

Thus, I dedicated myself to analyzing the media deconstruction of Paulo Freire's public image, through the use of fake news as technical instruments for the composition of false narratives in a mediatized communication strategy designed in two phases: tragedy and catharsis. Both of these are contained in what I called an everyday virtual-parallel reality; that is, a space in which the affective bond is the connector between faith, fear, hatred and everyday life. In this mediation, the discursive regency is given by the negationist context that operates disinformation as a political-ideological object.

In this way, two points connected to each other present themselves as generating devices of binding connections in the virtual-parallel space. They are 1) the affective bond, which infects such a space from the 'sensitive'[3]; and 2) the construction of a common, which is established from a market pedagogy structured in the sociocultural relations of its targets and in a null perspective of the education of people among themselves, 'mediated by the world'.[4]

---

3   Muniz Sodré, Antropológica do espelho: Uma Teoria da Comunicação Linear e em Rede, 2002.
4   Paulo Freire, Pedagogia do Oprimido, 1987, p.68.

These two moving and intertwined points are established and legitimized, as a binding action, in the dialogic affirmation of one in relation to the other. In other words, sensitive strategies legitimize the link raising a perspective of one useless education and the nullity of education is reaffirmed in the mediatized action of sensitive strategies.

In the tragedy phase, the articulation of media discourses is formulated by the narrative of corruption attributed to the *Partido dos Trabalhadores* (PT)[5] and by the explanation of the moral failure of education, given by the suggested subversiveness of the patron of Brazilian education, Paulo Freire.

In the catharsis, the *Operação Lava Jato*[6] [Operation Car Wash] emerges as an unfailing ethical institution capable of remedying the country's economic bankruptcy. In addition, it brings with it the idea of moral transformation of education through privatization, through the implementation of a conservative education based on prejudice, racial segregation, gender superiority and with the influence of religious dogmas of a neo-Pentecostal Christian character.

As a result, not only did I reorganize my actions as a professor, but I was able to formulate the basis for my doctoral research. It was when I understood, in the face of the strategic process of building false messages of demonization of the left, of the image of Paulo Freire and of education, that the ideological structures of these messages had as their central idea the deconstruction of an education model that could lead the student to "reading the world"[7] in order to transform it.

In this way, the choice of Paulo Freire by the right, as a representative of a "subjective and immoral" education to be denied, took place precisely because his ideas still represent one of the main resistances to the ideological structures of governments that try to maintain ignorance through an education without critical context, which makes the student a simple memorizer and repeater of words.

Freire is still the greatest representative of a literacy capable of promoting the individual to the fullness of their form, to a state of awareness and responsibility with oneself and with others. In addition, one comes to a learning capable of decoding reality, knowing it consciously and rewriting it. That is a way for the underprivileged to transform reality, as subjects of their own history.[8]

The current scenario is not healthy. The project of abandoning education to deterioration is making great strides. However, Paulo Freire's centenary seminar made me see that, even

---

5   Workers Party. A party that emerged as an agent promoting changes in the lives of city and rural workers, left-wing activists, intellectuals and artists. It was made official a political party on February 10, 1980, by the Superior Court of Electoral Justice and its main leader is Luiz Inácio Lula da Silva, known as Lula. Available at: https://pt.org.br/nossa-historia/.
6   Anti-corruption and money laundering initiative. It started in March 2014. Available at: http://www.mpf.mp.br/grandes-casos/lava-jato/entenda-o-caso.
7   Paulo Freire, Educação como prática da liberdade, 1967, p.5.
8   Paulo Freire, Pedagogia do Oprimido, p.30.

in the face of impossibilities, there is always a way out. There is always a ladder or a bridge. There is always someone able to step out of their comfort zone and reach out to you. And more, that after being pulled up, you understand the importance of this movement to continue to exist and, in this way, to make your hand a bridge to those who are in the place where you were before.

EPILOGUE: @PAULOFREIRE, 100 YEARS AND BEYOND?

ANA CRISTINA SUZINA AND THOMAS TUFTE

> We live in an age in which there is too much information, less knowledge and even
> less wisdom. That ratio needs to be reversed.
> We definitely need less information, more knowledge, and much more wisdom.
> Elif Shafak, How to stay sane in an age of division, 2020

When we started our most recent journey with Paulo Freire, it could be characterized as
an effort mainly to understand what made Freire such an ideal enemy for the emergent
conservative and right-wing government and movements in Brazil. It was early 2019 and,
together with César Jiménez-Martínez, a colleague from Cardiff University, we organized a
first seminar at Loughborough University London guided by the above question – particularly
puzzled by the election of Jair Bolsonaro to the Brazilian presidency in October of 2018.
That seminar led to a series of collective publications,[1] to new debates, and not least to the
seminar cycle and debates that are transcribed, edited and published in this book.[2] It also
led to our participation in some of many third parties' activities. This renewed focus upon,
and discussion of Paulo Freire's ideas, legacy and contemporary and future relevance was
intensified by the many celebrations of Freire's birth centennial throughout 2021.

In this epilogue, written in early 2022, we look back at this journey. What can we take from
such an intense series of celebrations and debates around the life and work of this Brazilian
adult educator? Is there a place and a role for Freire's thoughts in the current networked
society?

We have identified three main thematic threads amongst the numerous and diverse initiatives
we engaged in since March 2021: the first focuses on a sense of nostalgic celebration recalling
the life and work of Paulo Freire as an influential thinker of the 20th century; the second
suggests a new generation's engagement and a multidisciplinary move forward with Freire's

---

1   See 1) Dossier Paulo Freire, 100 anos. Revista Matrizes, v.15, n. 3 (octubre / diciembre de 2021):
    https://www.revistas.usp.br/matrizes.
    2) Special Issue 2020: The legacy of Paulo Freire. Roles and challenges of Social Movements. Commons.
    Revista de Comunicación y Ciudadanía Digital, 9(2): https://revistas.uca.es/index.php/cayp/issue/
    view/432https://revistas.uca.es/index.php/cayp/issue/view/432.
    3) Special Issue 2020: Freire's vision of development and social change – past experiences, present
    challenges and perspectives for the future. International Communication Gazette, 82: 5, August: https://
    journals.sagepub.com/toc/gazb/82/5.
    4) Suzina, A.C., Tufte, T. & Jiménez-Martínez, C. (2020). Qual a mensagem de Paulo Freire para os
    días atuais?: diálogos sobre a relevância do pensamento de Freire para entender o Brasil hoje. Revista
    Internacional de Comunicación y Desarrollo, 11, 11-18: https://revistas.usc.gal/index.php/ricd/article/
    view/6543.
2   Freire Centennial: 7 Talks in Preparation for the Next 100 Years: https://www.paulofreirecentennial.org/
    videos/.

ideas being rearticulated not only within fields where he is already influential but inspiring other disciplines and younger scholars and activists; the third and final thread addresses the emergence of new questions about the place of Freirean thought in an evolving, challenging and networked world. Each thematic thread will be unfolded in the following sections of this text.

However, before moving to these threads, allow us to highlight one transversal aspect that also justifies the inclusion of this book in the series 'Theory on Demand' of the Institute of Network Cultures. It relates to the process of defining the very sense of resistance or social change in the field of communication and media.

In her lecture during the cycle *Freire Centennial: 7 Talks in Preparation for the Next 100 Years*, in March 2021, Karin G. Wilkins, revealed her initial mixed feelings for being invited to talk about love.[3] Would it be appropriate and meaningful for a woman and feminist to give a lecture about love? She says, 'I was challenged by the idea of being invited to talk about love – as if a feminist should rather embrace contentious arguments and as if these could not contain love; as if love would not be the most contentious of all actions.'

Anita Gurumurthy also revealed an initial reticence in her process preparing her lecture about humility during the same cycle. Would it be relevant for a woman activist from India to talk about humility? In her words, 'we are so used to talk about the need of empowering voice that we do not look for humility.'

Their reflexivity recalls bell hooks' own questionings.

> Indeed, all the great movements for social justice in our society have strongly emphasized a love ethic. Yet young listeners remain reluctant to embrace the idea of love as a transformative force.[4]

The issue at stake here is that communication and social change activists, experts, practitioners and scholars may have been pushed by the urgency of increasing and accelerated global inequalities at many levels, as well as by equally increasing operational demands such as reaching efficiency, becoming more entrepreneurial, developing self-sustaining strategies for becoming independent from fundraising, turning actions and causes more visible and keeping updated with technological developments. All were pushed to the point where displaying affective features got questioned or simply dismissed. bell hooks, who was very inspired by Freire, called for us to return to love, and her book *all about love* is an elaborate vision of love's transformative power.

In this sense, recovering Paulo Freire through the intense celebrations of his birth centennial can be understood as reclaiming affect as resistance and as a core feature of social change. In opposition to hate, to distance and to cancellation, rearticulating a fine complementarity

---

3   In this book, Section 1.
4   bell hooks, All about love: new visions, 2001: p. xix.

between reason and affect becomes the cutting-edge reflection, and principles such as love, dialogue, empathy, humility and hope turn into fundamental aspects of a communication that wants itself to be emancipatory, no matter where and how is unfolds.

Recalling past struggles for social justice

Inevitably, a good number of participants at Freire's birth centennial celebrations recalled past experiences, thereby raising a nostalgic aspect. Part of these recollections constituted a sort of archaeological work, remembering Freire's endeavours as a man, as an educator and as a political actor, revisiting both his well-known and his lesser-known works in the process. In September 2021, the precise month of his birth centennial, Freire's book *Pedagogy of Oppressed* bounced back up of the list of bestsellers in Brazil, becoming the fifth most sold non-fiction book despite all hate campaigns organized against Freire by conservative movements in the country[5]. This renewed interest in Freire also played a role in articulating an engagement amongst younger audiences, who did not know him or previously knew very little of his work.

Globally, there is plenty of evidence of Freire's reach across the world. His works, mainly the *Pedagogy of Oppressed*, have been translated into more than 30 languages, and they are ranked as top references in both the field of education and more broadly in the social sciences. During the centennial celebrations, the global extent of his influence translated into numerous shared stories of memory and reinvention, evidenced both in this book, in the special issue of the Brazilian journal of communication, Matrizes,[6] and in many other publications.

An example of Freire's global reach is seen in how the leading Danish community media practitioner Birgitte Jallow read Freire back in the 1970s, and all the while she worked with feminist and other agendas, through her community media work in several countries across Asia, Africa and Europe, she unravels how her readings of Freire remained an undercurrent, a set of principles as it were, informing her way of working.[7] Similarly, Maria Celeste Cadiz, a renowned communication for development scholar from the Philippines has shared, in a co-authored piece, the experience of how Freire's works have been read and discussed for decades at University of the Philippines in Los Banos. Freire's ideas thereby informed numerous students and later practitioners of rural development work in the Philippines.[8] Another powerful story has been told by Jharna Brahma[9] about Freire's influence upon theatre for development movements in India. There, movements that still are very active and

---

5   According to Publishnews, a website specialized in the editorial market. See https://www.publishnews. com.br/materias/2021/10/01/no-seu-centenario-paulo-freire-volta-a-lista-dos-livros-mais-vendidos-do-publishnews.
6   Adilson Citelli, Ana Cristina Suzina and Thomas Tufte, *Dossier Paulo Freire, 100 anos*, Revista Matrizes, v.15, n. 3, octubre / diciembre de 2021.
7   See: Adilson Citelli, Ana Cristina Suzina and Thomas Tufte, 'Coexistence and Learning', Revista Matrizes, v.15, n. 3, october / december 2021.
8   Adilson Citelli, Ana Cristina Suzina and Thomas Tufte. 'Coexistence and Learning'.
9   See this book, Section 3.

relevant throughout the country, have drawn heavily on the Freire-inspired Forum Theatre work pioneered by Augusto Boal.

Beyond inspiring all these actors of social change, Freire was also seminal to South-South intellectual debates and dialogues on how to fight oppressors in the Global South. A particularly interesting example was seen in Ylva Gumede and Colin Chasi's accounts on how Freire inspired Steve Biko, a leading anti-apartheid activist in South Africa in the 1960s and 1970s and until he was murdered in 1977.[10]

In all these experiences, there is almost nothing about a direct reproduction of a method. The global spread of Freire's thoughts took form more as a conceptual or philosophical framework, and in dialogues with other local thinkers and practitioners who shared similar preoccupations and views of justice. The nostalgia about Freire experienced in these celebrations has thus been far from just nice recollection but have rather borne testimonials about Freire's humanity and about the dynamism permeating his philosophy of change.

These memories of Freire bear witness to social change processes in which 'Freire' more emerged as a meaningful conceptual framework that justified and endorsed the valorization of local knowledges in the construction of development solutions and political strategies. Freire did not come with a model to replace or discipline local practices but rather to emphasize their importance as a compulsory element of emancipation and/or social change. It relates well with the fact that many theoretical approaches built upon Freire's influence are charged with qualifications such as 'participatory' or 'horizontal', highlighting their bottom-up character. Revisiting these memories meant restoring the challenge of reinventing individual and collective practices through a close connection with the variety of contexts and diversity of local experiences.

New disciplines and new generations engaging with Freire

The multidisciplinary reach of Freire's thoughts could be observed by a particularly strong feature in the centennial celebrations: the diversity of voices of activists, scholars, students, and people from a broad gamut of research fields and of civil society struggles for social justice. From activists engaged in social movements since the struggle against the Brazilian military dictatorship (1964-1985) up to contemporary social movements such as the Landless Workers Movement in Brazil, people have shared insights about Freire's imprints upon their ideas, principles, visions and methods.

The digital magazine *Punto de Encuentro*, published by the association of Christian communicators *Signis ALC*, collected testimonials from Latin American educators,

---

10   Colin Chasi and Ylva Gumede, 'Critical Consciousness and Cultural Emancipation in (South) African Heritages of Communication for Social Change'. Revista Matrizes, v.15, n. 3, october / december 2021. Available at https://www.revistas.usp.br/matrizes/article/view/192718.

communication and human rights professionals and activists.[11] They recalled how meeting with Freire personally or with his ideas marked a turning point in their trajectories, both personally but also in the organizations and movements they worked in. These multiple voices have evidenced how Paulo Freire was a seminal and foundational inspirator to their way of working with processes of empowerment and with social change more broadly, pursuing processes of *conscientizacao* and social justice.

The centennial, however, did more than confirm the diverse and indeed global influence of Freire. It evidenced how new disciplines and new generations of scholars and activists are engaging with Freire's works and ideas.

This book has included a section in which 6 doctoral students, from India, South Africa, Tanzania, USA, Mexico and Brazil reflect upon how Freire has informed their research mainly within media and communication research, but also with some links to the field of education. For example, Nompumelelo Gumede critically assesses health communication practices in South Africa under the COVID crisis drawing on Freire's principles of empathy and dialogue. And Happy Singu Hansen uses Freirean thinking to identify limitations in Nyerere's educational policies in Tanzania, and at the same time discusses the Freirean inspired communication practices of a large youth-oriented NGO working within non-formal education. Many of these young communication scholars engaging with Freire use his ideas as a springboard from where to engage with and reflect upon both past and present communication practices of social movements, government agencies and civil society organizations.

Several, like both Michael Dokyum Kim and Fania Sanchez de la Vega González are also pointing towards the challenges of the digital future. In critically engaging with the 'new normal' of digitalization and online-communication evolving in the context of the COVID crisis, they are both drawing on Freire's ontological call to raise questions, cautioning the taken-for-grantedness of this new normality dominated by a technological determinism. In González' case, she argues that most likely Freire, had he lived, would 'invite us to re-think communication as a critical pedagogical tool'.[12] Kim is particularly concerned about the sectarian aspects of technocentrism, quoting Freire's distinction between sectarianism and radicalization: 'Sectarianism, fed by fanaticism, is always castrating. Radicalization, nourished by a critical spirit, is always creative. Sectarianism mythicizes and thereby alienates; radicalization criticizes and thereby liberates'.[13] Kim further argues that 'Datafied human agency exists to strengthen the power of algorithms, only to return to the social to be categorized in terms of race, gender, class, nationality, and the like. Algorithms, then mathematically decide what is normal and abnormal, further castrating the oppressed rather than liberating them.'[14]

---

11   Revista Punto de Encuentro, Revista Digital de SIGNIS ALC, available at https://signisalc.org/producto/ encuentros-paulofreire-comunicacion/.
12   This book, Section 3.
13   Paulo Freire, Pedagogy of the Oppressed, London: Penguin Books, 1996, p. 19.
14   This book, Section 3.

As we see in these reflections, a new generation of critical and activist oriented scholars are actively engaging with and inspired by Freirean thinking in communication and social change. They are using his philosophical framework for reflexive thinking and to engage critically with their time. We identified this new generation of critical scholars not only within the PhD students in Part III of this book but amongst many of the speakers during our own Centennial Celebrations and in many other of the events of this past year.

New scientific disciplines are also engaging with Freire's works and ideas. For example, when we both were invited to discuss communication for social change on an episode of *Disasters: Deconstructed*, a podcast organized for an international network of scholars in disaster research, we realized how Freire's ideas were inspiring debates about community resilience.[15] In the exchange with Jason von Meding and Ksenia Chmutina, two young scholars of disaster research who created and host the podcast, we reflected upon how the vulnerabilization of the people affected is as much constructed as the idea of disaster itself, creating victims without any agency over their experience or the possible solutions to come. Engaging with Freire brought up the centrality of a process of *conscientizacao* in this field, in order to place disasters within a broader context of social decisions regarding the management of natural and industrial resources, relationships with surrounding territories and peoples, and long-term perspectives.

Within critical design practices and their intersection with social movements there is a novel and growing orientation towards Latin American critical thinking, and Paulo Freire's work is central to their study. It can be seen in, for example, the works and talks of Frederik Van Amstel from the Federal University of Technology in Paraná, Brazil. As a Brazilian scholar of the young generation of critical design researchers, he has been instrumental in developing research network. In 2020, Frederick co-founded the Design & Oppression network and, in 2021, the Laboratory of Design against Oppression (LADO). It was quite clear that they are in the early stages of engaging with Freire, introducing him to the field of critical design research and practice along with scholars such as Frans Fanon and bell hooks.

Similarly, while not new, we have seen a renewed debate in public health research and practice. Freire has been inspiring generations of health communication scholars arguing for a broader social change-oriented agenda, transcending both the vision, conceptual framing and methods applied in health communication, critiquing the narrow individually oriented behaviour change models and arguing in favour of a deeper critical, participatory, bottom-up and social change oriented agenda. This debate has regained impetus in the context of the Covid pandemic. Gumede's South African example above is a case in point.

Furthermore, new generations of educators found in the centennial an occasion to revisit education in the context of current challenges. In commemorating Freire's birth centennial[16] the Faculty of Education of the University of Cambridge installed a sculpture of Paulo Freire.

---

15   The podcast can be accessed through any player, as here https://disastersdecon.podbean.com/e/s5e7-communication-for-social-change/.
16   See https://news.educ.cam.ac.uk/paulo-freire-sculpture-installed.

This happened during a large cycle of debates and exchanges about his legacy in education studies and practices. The gesture was presented as a symbol of resistance to attacks against education throughout the world, as well as a praise of dialogue. In Denmark, during the centennial year, a book was published on the pedagogy of hope and action as a pathway to critically engage children and youth in Danish schools around the sustainable development goals.[17] Thus, inspired by Freire, a new generation of Danish educators seek critically to engage a new generation of citizens in current challenges of development.

While new disciplines and new generations have been reflecting and acting upon Freirean thought, the field of communication has also been more broadly revisited during the centennial celebrations. We have seen a strong engagement of scholars and activists combining reviews of currently consolidated areas of studies and practices such as communication and education – or educommunication, as frequently named in Latin America – and popular communication. There has been a search for a broader ontological framework for communication and media based upon Freire's perspectives. A series of critical questions emerge from this search, as it is possible to see in the Part II of this book, pointing strongly to a discussion about the relevance of Freire in a networked society. Some of these questions are discussed in the next and final section.

New questions for an evolving world

Freire's birth centennial celebrations were mainly organized and experienced under the combination of a particular conjunction: the pandemics of Covid-19, an increased use of digital platforms that allowed much of human occupation and exchanges to keep going, and the emergence of conservative movements in several countries of the world. Almost inevitably, many participants of these celebrations were searching for some sort of inspiration as how to move forward in such a context. Questions that were raised in the debates included:

> Shall we have empathy towards the ultra-right? Is it possible to have dialogue within polarization, disinformation and hate speech? How to increase critical thinking under conservative governments? Is fake news building a fake history? How to combine a deep connection with local realities in a mediated world calling for globalization and involving deterritorialization? What is the place of oppressed people in the digital environment and how can we reach them? Can denunciation and announcement connect with the network society? How to build affectivity and critical thinking in fast forward education models, especially based in digital platforms? What to speak when we have voice and what about listening? Is it possible to resist and act for social change within this digital culture? What would Paulo Freire do? What would he make of this world?

---

17   A. Hojholdt and T. Ravn-Pedersen (eds), Haabets og Handlingens Paedagogik – undervisning I verdensmaal og baeredygtighed. Copenhagen: Hans Reitzels Forlag, 2021.

Looking particularly at the field of communication and media, we find it pertinent to conclude this epilogue by advancing some ideas coming from these debates about Freire's practices and works articulated in this year of celebration, but also moving beyond them. Freire used to ask people to reinvent instead of copying him, putting an emphasis upon stimulating dialogue with place, time and different social actors. The learnings from the Freire Centennial that we highlight below are inspired both by his seminal works, by the experiences of reinvention expressed by the recollections of so many scholars, practitioners, and activists in many fields, and by the challenges raised during these debates. We organize them in three categories: naming the world; being and remaining aware; resisting and re-existing.

NAMING THE WORLD

There is not a more ontological perspective of communication, from a Freirean perspective, than associating the capacity of naming things with the process of emancipating oneself and becoming an actor in society. It could not be more therapeutical either.

It is important to recognize that the frequency of questions raised within the large and diverse audience as that of the centennial celebrations suggests that experience with and concerns about hate speech, polarisation, limitations to education and action in digital environments exist and affect people all over the world. The global scale may, however, increase anxiety instead of helping to solve the challenges.

The oppressed, as a category, are not the same people in all places where Freire's thoughts are applied. Emancipation does not mean the same either. The strength of these notions, in Freire's work, is that they push people to identify the forces of oppression and the resources available to face and fight it. Naming the dimension of polarization, identifying the actors involved in hate speech and understanding the dynamics through which people engage with digital networks in each context may bring the problem to a scale where action becomes possible and hope, reachable.

BEING AND KEEPING AWARE

Ailton Krenak made a bonus participation, after his lecture, that offers a provoking perspective.[18] He said, '...this speech, which is virtual, refers to another maneuver that we are undergoing: that of admitting that there is a screen between us and pretending that there is not.' He is discussing the imposed technology mediation and its effect upon the way our society understands – or needs to understand – connection beyond digital connectivity.

The provocation brings us back to Freire's notion of *conscientizacao*. The naturalization of the networked society builds an idea that there is no alternative form, or that the digital networks are the alternative *per se*. Although recognizing the affordances of screens – that indeed

18   This book, Section 1.

made possible an exchange with Krenak from his indigenous community in Brazil – the idea of being aware of it invites us to remain awake and, consequently, able to both enjoy the benefits as well as to criticize the risks that any technology may introduce into our societies. In this globally marketed human society, we can assume that Freire would invite us, as Gonzalez suggests, to re-think communication as a critical pedagogical tool.[19]

RESISTING AND RE-EXISTING

Would Paulo Freire be on social networks? He used to say that he would accept any invitation to talk on the media as long as it was a live participation, because he found it was his role to 'occupy' the spaces that were not naturally assigned to him. As González suggested, 'it is not about cancelling the digital media, but about giving them their rightful place'.[20] Re-existing in digital networks is, then, about resisting the naturalization of the idea that humans must adapt to a digital architecture imposed by a few; it is instead about insisting that this architecture must be at the service of a diverse society and flexible enough to connect with other communication architectures more appropriate to a variety of realities, needs and wills.

Revisiting Freire's ideas in relation to communication leads us to remember the fact that communication and media constitute a platform but are more than just that. We have all long been witnessing and awaiting, but also critically engaging in, the development of a new order in information and communication. The network society has laid a technological ground with the digital media delivering affordances. However, a new world information and communication order (NWICO), to paraphrase the debates of the 1970s and 1980s, may well be networked and digital, as long as it engages with the principle of dialogue. It must include the dialogue between the abundance of technologies and all the emancipatory, participatory and historically developed strategies and it must allow subjectivity and agency to flourish and to syntonize with the pace of transformations required. If this core Freirean principle and process is not deeply part of the change, the new order may well be part of the oppression.

---

19   See above.
20   This book, Section 3.

BIOGRAPHIES

Ailton Krenak is an Indigenous human rights activist, born in 1953, in the *Doce* River Valley, Brazil, belonging to the Krenak ethnic group. In 1987, he led the struggle for several principles inscribed in the Federal Constitution of Brazil. He founded and leads the *Núcleo de Cultura Indígena*, and created the *Festival de Danças e Culturas Indígenas*. Journalist, presenter of the series *Índios no Brasil* for TV Educativa in 1998, and the series with indigenous thematic *Tarú Andé* for TV Futura in 2007. Author of texts and articles published in collections in Brazil and abroad. He was awarded the title of *Professor Honoris Causa* by the Federal University of Juiz de Fora-UFJF and received several prestigious national and international awards.

Ana Cristina Suzina is a Leverhulme Early Career Fellow in the Institute for Media and Creative Industries at Loughborough University London. Her research deals with youth appropriation of media and generational factors over the development of views of development, political imagination, and political voice. Her research interests include social change, power asymmetries, media appropriation, participation in democracy, civil society development, grassroots communication, particularly focused in Latin American societies. Suzina is the editor of the book The Evolution of Popular Communication in Latin America (Palgrave, 2021).

Anita Gurumurthy is founding member and executive director of IT for Change (ITfC), where she leads research on emerging issues in the digital context such as the platform economy, data and AI governance, democracy in the digital age and feminist frameworks on digital justice. She also directs ITfC's field resource centre that works with grassroots rural communities on 'technology for social change' models. Anita actively engages in national and international advocacy on digital rights and contributes regularly to academic and media spaces.

Benjamin Ferron is a French sociologist, PhD in Political Science, Lecturer in Political Communication at East-Paris University (Céditec EA 3119), member of the Media Sociology Network (AFS-RT37) and adjunct researcher at the CENS (UMR 6025). He teaches and conducts research in sociology of journalism, social movements media, communication for social change, public problems, field theory and methodology of social sciences. He publishes in French, English and Spanish. His current projects include the books Giving Voice to the "Voiceless"? Social and discursive construction of a Public Problem (with E. Née & C. Oger, 2022), Political sociology: the Media Communication of Social Movements (forthcoming) and Sociology of the French Free Media Movement (forthcoming).

Claudia Magallanes-Blanco is a Professor in the Department of Humanities at Universidad Iberoamericana Puebla, Mexico, where she co-founded the master's in communication and Social Change. She holds a PhD in Humanities from University of Western Sydney, Australia, and a specialization on Epistemologies of the South by the Latin American Council on Social Sciences (CLACSO). An academic and activist for social justice, she has been working with collectives and organizations concerned with community and Indigenous communication for more than 15 years. Together with Charlotte Ryan and Alice Mattoni, she is coeditor of the Routledge book series *Media and Communication Activism: The Empowerment Practices of Social Movements*.

Colin Chasi is Professor and Director of the Unit for Institutional Change and Social Justice at the University of the Free State, in South Africa. He writes on the decolonization of the discipline. With grounding in quintessential African thought, he is pursuing what he terms Participation Studies.

Elijerton Veras was born in 1974, in São Benedito (Ceará), Brazil. He is currently a teacher of young people from the periphery and young offenders in compliance with socio-educational measures at Senac-RJ. He is also a Lecturer/Tutor of postgraduate/MBA courses at Fundação Getúlio Vargas. Graduated in Social Communication from Universidade Estácio de Sá (UNESA), he is a current doctoral student in Social Communication with emphasis on Media and Everiday Life at Universidade Federal Fluminense, and a member of Laccops/UFF (Research Laboratory in Community Communication and Social Advertising). Elijerton studies education and politics, their relationships with the hegemonic and counter-hegemonic media and their impacts on everyday life, as well as Social Advertising articulated to social movements and Human Rights.

Eriberto Gualinga Montalvo is director of documentaries, photography, and music in the defense of the Amazon region and human rights. He has been working with audiovisuals for 20 years and his works have been exhibited in many festivals around the world, winning the *Paco Urondo* and the *National Geographic* prizes, among other recognitions.

Fania Sánchez de la Vega González is a communicator, educator, and social researcher. She holds a master's in Communication and Social Change from Universidad Iberoamericana Puebla, in Mexico, which contributed to strengthen her critical perspective on the human world. She was a professor in the areas of humanities, social sciences, and language for five years. In the past three years, she worked with two NGOs in Mexico, the first is dedicated to the education of vulnerable youth and the second uses dialogue and urban art as tools for change. As a researcher, she's interested in migration, social movements, and youth. In 2018, she published an article on technopolitics, collective action and the undocumented immigrant youth movement in USA. She loves teaching, but mostly, she loves learning.

Frei Betto is a Dominican friar and writer, author of 70 books, many of them translated in multiple languages. He received several awards, in Brazil and abroad, for his fight for human rights – such as the *Dom Paulo Evaristo Arns Award*, the *Medalla Universidad Nacional* from the Universidad Nacional de Costa Rica, and the *Medal of the National Order of Merit*, in the Grade of Officer, from Ecuador. Frei Betto was also awarded with the title of *Doctor Honoris Causa* from the University of Habana (Cuba) and from José Martí University (Mexico). He is currently a member of the World Council of the José Martí Project for International Solidarity and an adviser to Food and Agricultural Organization (FAO), the UN agency for Food Security and Nutrition Education.

Happy Singu Hansen is a Doctoral researcher at Loughborough University London, United Kingdom. With her research, she aims to analyse the longitudinal perspectives of the work by a major player in youth empowerment work in Tanzania; the civil society organisation Femina. Happy also co-initiated the organisation 'IPSI' aiming to develop civic and social entrepreneurial activities among youth in Tanzania.

James Deane is Head of Policy at BBC Media Action, the charity set up by the BBC to support media around the world and advance international development. He is also currently working as a consultant to Luminate, a philanthropic foundation, to develop an International Fund for Public Interest Media.

Jharna Brahma is a Doctoral researcher at the University of Hyderabad, India. She studies a social change initiative of the local people based in West Bengal in India, facilitated mainly by Augusto Boal's 'Theatre of the oppressed' technique, which was inspired by Paulo Freire's Pedagogy of the Oppressed. She has worked in the public health sector in India and then as a researcher in association with the UNESCO Chair, Community Media, UoH and RMIT University, Australia. Her research interest lies in the role of human's intrinsic resources like love and compassion in the social change politics. She is also interested in studying social movements, participatory, innovative, alternative approaches to communication, development and social change. Her most recent publication is *Driving Social Change Through Forum Theatre: A Study of Jana Sanskriti in West Bengal, India*, 2019.

Karin Gwinn Wilkins has a PhD from the University of Pennsylvania and is the Dean of the School of Communication at the University of Miami. Previously, she was Associate Dean for Faculty Advancement and Strategic Initiatives with the Moody College of Communication at the University of Texas at Austin. She was awarded the *Cale McDowell Award for Innovation in Undergraduate Studies*. Wilkins is also a recognized fellow of the International Communication Association (ICA) and has concluded her term as Editor-in-Chief of *Communication Theory*. She has won numerous awards for her research, service, and teaching, currently serving as Vice-President of the Arab-US Association for Communication Education. Her most recent book with University of California Press is *Prisms of Prejudice: Mediating the Middle East from the United States* (2021).

Linje Manyozo is a student of the human condition, whose praxis involves demobilizing the pervasiveness of the emperor's phallus as a way to undermine the discourses and structures of inequality. In his idealism, Linje' work, informed by liberatory theology, places God at the centre of the subaltern's efforts to integrate citizen voices in development policy formulation and implementation. Currently, Dr Linje Manyozo teaches in RMIT's College of Design and Social Context. He has published three books: *Communicating Development with Communities* (Routledge, 2017); *Media, Communication and Development* (Sage, 2013) and *People's Radio* (Southbound, 2012). His latest work, *Wisdom of Water* (2022), celebrates God and indigenous wisdom as foundation stones for working with people. Linje's people-centred work is summarised in *Pedagogy of Listening*, where he emphasizes that development is about working with God so as to make love to people.

Mayrá Lima has a PhD in Political Science from the University of Brasília and is a journalist. She is a member of the communication sector of the Landless Rural Workers Movement / MST-Brasil. She researches the political behavior of rural elites in Brazil and issues related to communication and democracy, social movements and participation.

Michael Dokyum Kim is a Doctoral Candidate in the School of Communication at University of Miami; he earned an MSc in Media, Communication and Development from the London School of Economics and Political Science. His research interests relate to communication for social change, digital development, and representations of development cooperation.

Nompumelelo 'Mpume' Gumede is a PhD Candidate at the Centre for Communication, Media and Society (CCMS) at the University of KwaZulu-Natal, South Africa. Her research interests are in Social and Behaviour Change Communication (SBCC), with a special focus on bottom-up approaches to Health Communication. Nompumelelo's current PhD study explores a people's science to COVID-19 communication in township, rural and informal settlements in South Africa. Her study locates culture as central to the development of locally-relevant COVID-19 communication.

Thomas Tufte is Director of Institute for Media and Creative Industries at Loughborough University London, and Extraordinary Professor at University of The Free State, South Africa. He is member of Academia Europaea. Tufte works on the role of communication in articulating citizen engagement and social change, mainly as a researcher, but also as a consultant to international development agencies and as practitioner. He has worked, lectured and researched in over 30 countries across mainly Latin America, Africa and Europa. His most recent books include *Voice and Matter – Communication, Development and the Cultural Return*, co-edited with Oscar Hemer (Nordicom, 2016) *Communication and Social Change – a Citizen Perspective* (Polity Press, 2017), and *Communicating for Change – Concepts to think with*, co-edited with Jo Tacchi (Palgrave, 2020).

Xavier Carbonell is a writer and journalist, graduated in Hispanic Philology, from the Universidad Central "Marta Abreu" de Las Villas, Cuba. He has a Diploma in Modern and Contemporary Philosophy from the Pontificia Universidad Católica de Chile, and a Laudato Si' Certificate in Compassion and Social Communication, from the Xavier University of Bhubaneshwar, India. He works as a correspondent for SIGNIS, the World Catholic Association for Communication, and participated in the SIGNIS Communication Laboratory based in Quito, Ecuador. He worked as a researcher and teacher for the Manuel García-Garófalo Diocesan Library in Santa Clara, Cuba, where he founded the Academic Project Humanitas. He was awarded with the Foundation Award of the City of Santa Clara, Cuba, for his novel *El libro de mis muertos*, and the Paco Rabal Award of Cultural Journalism from AISGE Foundation, Spain, for his article *Cuba in seven films*. Recently, he received the XXV City of Salamanca Novel Award, for *El fin del juego*. He lives in exile in Salamanca, Spain.

www.ingramcontent.com/pod-product-compliance
Lightning Source LLC
Chambersburg PA
CBHW022337280326
41934CB00006B/673